▷ REMODELING ORGANIZER ◁

Robert Irwin

Real Estate
Education Company
® a division of Dearborn Financial Publishing, Inc.

While a great deal of care has been taken to provide accurate and current information, the ideas, suggestions, general principles and conclusions presented in this text are subject to local, state and federal laws and regulations, court cases and any revisions of same. The reader is thus urged to consult legal counsel regarding any points of law—this publication should not be used as a substitute for competent legal advice.

Acquisitions Editor: Christine E. Litavsky
Managing Editor: Jack Kiburz
Interior Design: Lucy Jenkins
Cover Design: Paul Perlow Design

Library of Congress Cataloging-in-Publication Data

Irwin, Robert, 1941–
      The home remodeling organizer / Robert Irwin.
            p.   cm.
      Includes index.
      ISBN 0-7931-1337-7
      1. House buying.   2. House selling.   3. Dwellings—Remodeling—
Economic aspects.   I. Title.
      HD1390.5.I788   1995
      643'.7—dc2094-48599

                                                                              CIP

Contents

Preface

I love remodeling homes.

I've been doing it for more than 30 years and usually, though not always, I make money on the work. Sometimes, if I've done my homework well, I make a lot of money. Other times, I pay for my expenses and make a modest profit. Once or twice, things have gone sour and I've lost money.

I suspect that's the way it is with most businesses. However, the appeal for me isn't just the chance at a hefty profit (although that's certainly a strong motivation). The bigger incentive is that I really love to work with older, run-down properties. I like figuring out what needs to be done to turn a property around. I enjoy remodeling a kitchen or rebuilding a bath. I don't mind carefully painting a door or adding a deck. I also like living in many different homes, something that is a real plus in remodeling.

In short, unless I'm working with my hands on a remodeling project, I don't feel as if I'm contributing something worthwhile. When I am working, even if I put in long days and have some aches and pains in the evening, I'm content.

My purpose in telling you this is that I believe it's the real secret for success in remodeling. It's not necessary to do it full-time; you can work on weekends or evenings. It's not necessary to be a world-class carpenter, plumber or tile-layer. (I'm certainly not!) It's not even necessary to find spectacular bargains.

What is necessary is to enjoy doing the work. If you can look at a run-down ruin of a property and in your mind's eye visualize the grand home that it could be; if you can hardly wait to get your hands on a hammer, saw and screwdriver and get to work; if you relish living in a home that you've remodeled with your own hands, then I guarantee that, one way or another, you'll make a success of remodeling.

Organizing Your Remodeling

Home remodeling can mean something small, such as putting a new sink in a bathroom. Or it can mean something very big, such as completely rehabilitating a broken-down house—a whole house rehabilitation (rehab). For most people, remodeling lies somewhere in between.

In this book we'll cover how to organize the entire spectrum of remodeling projects. In earlier chapters we'll see what it takes personalitywise to remodel and how to organize specific tasks. In later chapters we'll emphasize working with fixer-uppers, where the idea is buying at a very low price then spending time and elbow grease at cleaning and fixing up and, finally, selling for a healthy profit.

In short, we'll cover the following areas:

- Remodeling projects large to small

- Judging which remodeling projects make financial sense

- Buying a fixer-upper, rehabilitating it and reselling for a profit

- Renovating your current home into the place you know it can be

- Going into business for yourself by regularly buying, remodeling and then selling properties for profit

■ THE ULTIMATE DECISION

Should you remodel? Or should you not? This is the ultimate choice you're going to have to make. Over and again in this book, the criterion used to make this decision is going to be *value*. Does the work you're going to do make financial sense? Will you add enough value to the property by the remodeling job to make it worthwhile doing?

If it doesn't add value, then it's probably not worth doing, even if you think you're doing it just for fun. (Remember, most people in this country move every seven to nine years. You'll probably be thinking about selling that home of yours sooner than later—and then the value added by remodeling will become a very important consideration.)

■ GETTING ORGANIZED

The real problem for most people, regardless of the size of the remodeling task, is getting organized. You may have the will, but do you have the way? Although the impulse is frequently there, the worst thing a would-be remodeler can do is simply to start tearing things apart. You know you want to put in a new window, so you begin hacking at the wall. You know you want a new countertop, so you begin smashing out the old tiles.

I know the feeling. You want to get started somewhere—to get a handle on the job—and the easiest course seems to be to tear down the old.

Don't do it. It's a mistake. The first tool you need is not a hammer, but a pencil. If there's one most important thing to remember from this book, it's that you must first pencil out the job. It's another way of saying "think before you act."

Regardless of the job's size, home remodeling makes sense only if the results justify the effort. It doesn't really matter if you're redoing a kitchen, adding a deck or planting shrubs. Whatever project you do must make sense on at least two levels:

1. *Financial sense.* Whether you intend to rehab a whole house for the quick sale or put in a new bathroom counter in your own

home, you don't want to waste money. You want to be sure that, at the least, your costs will be returned by an equal increase in the value of the property. (If you're in it for the quick return, you want to be sure that the property is worth more when you're finished than when you start.)

2. *Personal satisfaction.* The other big reason for remodeling is that you like doing it. A large percentage of the population, men and women, are tinkerers and doers. We (I include myself in this group) love to fix up things, especially property.

My suggestion is that if you don't have at least a spark of enthusiasm for doing the actual work, you may want to reconsider remodeling. In Chapter 2 we'll go into whether you have the aptitude. But even before that, it's important to know that you have the desire. A love of working with your hands, of building things, of making them more beautiful and more functional is necessary for real success in home remodeling. In other words, I discourage you from attempting it simply for the money. In fact, I know of no successful person who has made a career out of doing something he or she doesn't like.

On the other hand, don't let personal satisfaction blind you to the need that a project should make financial sense. I've never known anyone who loved to play poker, for example, yet liked to lose. I've never known a remodeler, no matter how much he or she liked to putter, who enjoyed doing all the work but liked losing money on the project. A major theme of this book will be to convince you to do only those projects that make financial sense.

REMODELING SUCCESS FORMULA

Positive result = Effort + Financial sense + Personal satisfaction

■ WHAT IS INVOLVED IN REMODELING?

Here's a list of some of the things that a remodeler may be called upon to do:

- Clean, paint and wallpaper
- Put in landscaping
- Add or join rooms
- Modernize bathrooms and kitchens
- Build decks
- Deal with workers
- Buy and sell fixer-uppers
- Handle bookkeeping and accounting
- Create additions
- Work on foundations
- Repair floors
- Work with banks or other lenders
- Repair plumbing or electrical
- Fix roofs
- Make money on resale

Of course, remodelers do not necessarily do all of the work themselves. Some people, in fact, never lift a hammer or drive a nail; some never get their hands dirty. Their joy is in figuring out how to do the job, in organizing and directing the workers, or in handling the finances. In fact, much of the important work involves making decisions based on calculations. The more accurate your figures and the better your judgment, the more successful you will be.

■ HOME REMODELING DECISIONS

In short, home remodeling can be more mental than physical. To show you why, here's a list of some decisions you may need to make:

- Is a property suitable for fixing up?

- What's the right kind of purchase and appropriate financing?

- What is a property's true potential (expansion, repair, yard versus house, etc.)?

- What should be rehabilitated, and what should be left as is?

- Should only cosmetic work be done or should real repairs and improvements be made?

- When should you do the work yourself, and when should you pay a professional?

- How much will it cost? Do the costs justify the work?

- How should the work be scheduled—where and when should the money be spent?

- When should you sell or refinance for a profit?

■ DOING IT YOURSELF

Although you may hire out some of the work, chances are that doing it yourself may be the only way to make a real profit in most home remodeling projects.

Just keep in mind, however, that to remodel a property successfully you do have to become personally involved. That means either physically working on the job or mentally planning and hiring others to execute your plan—or some combination of both. Perhaps the greatest mistake that any would-be remodeler can make is to think that he or she can do it as a nonparticipant.

You can't be a silent investor. On small projects, if you simply call in someone to do all the work for you, chances are you'll spend a fortune and will overimprove your property, so that the remodeling is a money loser. On rehabs, if you buy a property and then hire someone else, such as a general contractor (GC), to do all of the work, chances are you won't make money. The GC, not you, will make the profit. The bottom line is that remodeling is not a spectator sport!

■ DIFFERENCES BETWEEN A HOME REMODELER AND A CONTRACTOR

If you think many of the decisions a home remodeler makes are similar to those of a contractor, you're right. Both intend to make money on the work. However, there are a few differences.

- The home remodeler almost always does it part-time on purpose. The contractor tries to work full-time.

- The contractor usually looks at it strictly as work. The rehabber sees it also as play.

- The contractor mostly does it for other people. The rehabber does it for his or her own rewards.

■ REMODELING FOR PROFIT

Chances are you're not going to make a big profit by putting a new shower in your bathroom. However, there is serious money to be made if you move into the field of rehabilitating run-down homes. For a few moments, let's consider rehabbing (dealt with at length beginning with Chapter 10).

My first experience with rehabbing was in 1959. I bought a house in San Jose, California; it was a complete mess. I paid close to $6,000 for the property. (Real estate prices back then weren't what they are now!)

The foundation had settled, so the house had to be jacked up and straightened. The bathroom and kitchen had to be torn out and replaced. The floors had to be redone, and a new entrance had to be added. And there was a lot more work to be done. However, back then costs weren't high, and everything was done for around $4,000. I sold the house for $13,500 within two months of buying it.

It doesn't take a mathematical whiz to realize that I made a $3,500 profit. Now a $3,500 profit may not seem like much today, but my profit was close to 60 percent of what I paid for the building. Since I had borrowed all but a thousand dollars, the profit was a 350 percent return on my investment—in just two months!

These sorts of big profits are what the remodeler who is into rehabbing is looking for. In fact, some people who rehab will not buy a property unless they can foresee a 50 percent increase in the home's value and a 100 percent profit on their investment in less than six months!

In some exclusive, older areas of cities across the country, for example, some people have become professional rehabbers. They buy smaller, older homes. Then they add on to the shell of the old home, sometimes more than doubling the square footage. When they're finished, the result is a home that looks like new, is large and modern, and commands an enormous price. The fact that they continue to do this year in and year out proves that profits are there. (In talking with several of these professional rehabbers from the San Fernando Valley, Los Angeles, I found that the profits on such projects usually vary from a low of about $50,000 to a high of $250,000!)

Note: Throughout this book I refer to my personal experience remodeling houses in California. Real estate values are high in our state, and prices I quote should not be taken as a national norm. You may be able to accomplish the same thing with much less money in other parts of the country.

Risks in Total Home Remodeling

There are also risks in remodeling. This realization came to me in a big way with the second home I attempted to completely remodel (rehab), back in 1960. This was a house built before the turn of the century. It didn't even have a concrete foundation but instead had a true mudsill. The builder had watered the ground and then laid redwood (because it deteriorates slowly) on the mud and built the house up from there. The walls had no framing; they were instead two 1-inch-thick planks, 18 inches wide, nailed to each other diagonally. The plumbing and electrical systems were ancient.

Over time, everything had settled this way and that, and the house looked like a badly built toy. I bought it for $5,000, the price of the lot, which was zoned for duplexes. Shortly after I bought it, I found a note tacked to the door from the local building department. Apparently, they had been after the previous owner to bring the house up to the building code. He had "neglected" to inform me of this.

Because I was just getting started, and rather green, I thought that I could arrange a compromise with the building department. A conference with them convinced me otherwise. There was no alternative but to bring the house up to code. I soon discovered that it would be cheaper to bulldoze the existing house and build a new house from scratch! In short, the home could not effectively be rehabbed.

As I said, I was green and thus hadn't done my homework properly. Needless to say, I was depressed. I stood to lose all of the money I had invested.

But I didn't lose any money. Remember, the lot was zoned for duplexes. I had the old house bulldozed and, in partnership with a builder, put up a duplex that was later sold for a substantial profit. If you buy right when you rehab, even a loss can turn out to be a gain!

■ HOME REMODELING INSIGHTS

I hope this discussion has given you some insights into what home remodeling involves. I've personally been doing it for 30 years. The projects I've done include simple things such as painting and wallpapering, intermediate things such as putting in a new kitchen or bath, and really big things, such as rebuilding an entire house.

In this book I've tried to put down everything I've learned over that time in the hope that it will help you get organized, move along quickly and, perhaps most important, save a lot of money.

CHAPTER 2

Can *You* Remodel Homes?

Why get involved in remodeling homes? The obvious answers are that it's fun and it can be profitable. I want to reemphasize that fun and making money go hand in hand. Although a lot of profit can be made in home remodeling, you really must love what you do in order to succeed. And even if you are truly turned on to what you're doing, if you waste money and lose a bundle when you sell, you're not going to be happy.

In this chapter we're going to look at how well suited you are to remodeling. Is it the sort of thing you really want and can do? In short, we're going to organize your personal outlook. We're going to assess your remodeling aptitude.

■ WHAT HOME REMODELING OFFERS

Remodeling homes can offer you at least five different benefits. Do these fit in with your own personal wants and needs?

The Chance To Build Things

Some people are born builders. We like to build anything from model planes to computers. If you're this sort of person, you will typically have one or two projects on the back burner. In fact, you don't really feel comfortable, no matter what else you do in life, unless there's something you can get your hands on to fix or to rebuild.

Since the best way to remodel is to do the work yourself (it's far more profitable, and you get total control), remodeling offers you the chance to get out there and sweat a little while satisfying your urge to build. Most of the really successful remodelers I know do much of the work themselves, even when they can easily afford to hire it out. They prefer doing it themselves. It gives them a good feeling to be making something with their hands.

Be Your Own Boss

Thoreau said that most people "lead lives of quiet desperation." And most people work for someone else their entire lives. Working for someone else means that you are told what to do, where to do it and when. The big decisions are made for you, not by you.

This is not to say that there's anything wrong with working for someone else. If that someone is a large corporation, for example, the benefits of a large salary, health insurance, retirement and so forth can be substantial. On the other hand, there's the matter of your ego. Wouldn't you like to be the person in charge? Wouldn't you like to take risks and, when you're successful, reap the profits? Wouldn't you like to create your own ideas and see them carried out without being shot down by a supervisor? Wouldn't you like to say, "It's going to be done this way, because I say so!"?

I daresay that most of us would. And remodeling for profit and fun offers us the chance to do so. If you decide to remodel a kitchen and put in pine cabinets instead of oak, no one is going to tell you otherwise. You don't have to justify your costs, your ideas or your work to anyone but yourself—or to the ultimate buyer of the property.

The fact that you have to resell at some time to make your profit (you can also refinance to get your money out, as we'll see shortly) means that you do have to please a buyer. But that leaves a lot of room for creativity, which is just what home remodeling offers you: the chance to create your own work, to be in charge, to be your own boss.

Earn Extra Income

As I said at the beginning of this chapter, people remodel for fun and for profit. Two common types of home remodelers are investors, who are originally motivated by profit, and tradespeople or handy-persons, who want to increase their income during slack periods. Home remodeling offers them a chance to earn extra income while continuing with their regular jobs.

When you buy a house that needs remodeling or you begin some other remodeling project, you usually plan on several months during which you would work in the evenings, on weekends and when you have time available from your other job. In short, you do it in your spare time. Does earning income in your spare time appeal to you? If so, home remodeling offers that benefit.

Tax Deductions

When you own property and fix it up, certain tax deductions may be available to you that you would not get as a salaried worker. For example, as a profitable businessperson, you may be able to deduct an office in your home, equipment that you purchase for your work, and time and car expenses relating to the remodeling project. (The deductions are generally available only to be subtracted from your profits. You cannot reasonably expect to lose money in a side occupation and get deductions for it as well.) In addition, if you remodel a whole house, all the costs of acquiring the property may become deductible either annually or when you sell. A good accountant is invaluable in pointing out the deductions that may be available to you. (See Chapter 13 for additional information.)

A Bargain Home

Finally, there's the great American pastime of acquiring property. As we all know, even in a bad market, real estate of all kinds is expensive. Often we can't afford to buy the home we want.

Home remodeling offers the chance to get into a much better house than you might otherwise afford. Instead of paying top dollar for a house that's all in great shape, you pay bottom dollar for a so-called fixer-upper.

This book gives you the techniques you need to find fixer-uppers and put them back into shape. You may not want to sell for a profit, but instead simply live in the home.

■ THE DOWNSIDE OF HOME REMODELING

Almost everyone has a secret desire or fantasy. One of the most common that I've observed in people is to run a successful restaurant. For some reason almost everyone seems to think that they would make a great restaurateur.

I assume it's the thought of serving truly marvelous meals to other people that's so appealing. Perhaps we see ourselves in a tuxedo or evening dress escorting elegant customers to tables set with linen and antique silverware. Or it may be impressing others with our knowledge of vintage wines. Or it may be preparing and serving ethnic meals that we loved as children and now hunger for as adults.

Whatever the fantasy, the reality is almost always jarringly different. The restaurant business is tough and competitive at all levels, and most who go into it without extensive background, particularly in finance, fail. Chances are that if one of your secret goals is to be a great restaurateur—forget it. The statistics show that you would fail at great expense. You might end up with a little beanery, working for slave wages and hating every moment of it.

To a lesser degree, a similar problem prevails in home remodeling, although far more people can succeed at home remodeling than at restaurateuring. Looking at the benefits described earlier, a person might say, "Yes, that's just the thing for me!" It's not all benefits, however. The fantasy is big profits in real estate for doing simple work you love to do. The reality can be quite different. Home remodeling can involve months of hard, tedious work; working with people whom you discover you don't particularly like; discovering only at the end that the work didn't turn out as planned; realizing that you bought a property so far away that you must commute too far and thus have difficulty controlling the work; and facing financial hardship, even ruin, as a project goes over budget.

I'm not trying to scare you. I'm simply pointing out that home remodeling, like any endeavor, also has a downside. Simply loving the work and anticipating the profits won't cut the mustard. You also have to be prepared for the hard knocks.

■ HOW TO SUCCEED

As I noted earlier, the way to succeed in home remodeling is to love doing it and to have the skills needed. Here are two self-tests you can take. The first will examine your attitude. Do you really love doing remodeling work or are you kidding yourself? The second will ask you if you have the skills needed. Keep in mind that skills can be learned, but it can be very hard to change an attitude.

Testing Your Attitude

Your best chance of avoiding most of the problems that home remodeling holds, in my opinion, is to be truly suited to the work. I've found that if people love doing something for the money and actually down deep dislike it, they'll find a way to fail.

Note that there is no "official" attitude test for determining the successful remodeler. The field isn't so large that researchers have spent time coming up with a perfect profile.

Figure 2.1 is a simple little test based on the personality profiles of people I have known to be successful in home remodeling over the past 30 years. Scoring low does not mean you will fail. Scoring high does not guarantee you will succeed. This test is simply one additional piece of input to help make your own decision about whether or not to try home remodeling.

The test is not scientific. In fact, its purpose is to give you some insight into what you might face as a remodeler. The more times you answer yes, the better your chance of succeeding. A score of 17 or more in the Yes column is a definite indication that home remodeling could be for you; 14 to 17 indicates you'll probably like it; 13 and lower suggests that maybe you'd be better off trying your hand at another job.

FIGURE 2.1 ■ Home Remodeling Attitude Test

	Yes	No
1. Do you know how things work without being shown?	☐	☐
2. Do you like to work with your hands?	☐	☐
3. Do you like to solve problems on your own?	☐	☐
4. When entering an unfamiliar house are you more interested in how it's built than in the furnishings?	☐	☐
5. Are you interested in architecture?	☐	☐
6. If a faucet leaks in your home, do you fix it yourself rather than call a plumber?	☐	☐
7. If an electrical plug shorts out, do you fix it yourself rather than call an electrician?	☐	☐
8. Do you like doing your own accounting?	☐	☐
9. Do you feel better when there's no one supervising your work?	☐	☐
10. Are you willing to explain to other people what you want done, understanding that if they fail at the task, the loss will come out of your pocket?	☐	☐
11. Do you like putting on coveralls and getting your hands dirty working on a project?	☐	☐
12. Do you like negotiating and haggling over prices?	☐	☐
13. Would you rather work on your car than go to a movie?	☐	☐
14. Do you find it easy to schedule your time on weekends?	☐	☐
15. Do you seldom, if ever, wake up at night worrying about decisions you made the day before?	☐	☐
16. Do others think that you made good business judgments in the past?	☐	☐
17. Do you avoid making impulsive decisions and instead carefully think things out in advance?	☐	☐
18. Are you a patient person?	☐	☐
19. Do you get along well with tradespeople?	☐	☐
20. Have you always had a secret desire to build your own home?	☐	☐

Aptitude and Skills

I've always wanted to fly a plane on my own. Someday I'll probably do it. However, I wouldn't advise you to come along as a passenger, at least not at first. Regardless of my desire, I may have no talent for piloting. And until I spend a lot of time cracking the books and taking lessons, I have no skill at it whatsoever. In short, simply because I may have the temperament to be a great pilot doesn't mean I'll make one.

Let's see if you have some of the skills you'll need to succeed as a remodeler. Of course, no simple test such as this can truly measure your aptitude or ability to learn a skill. However, I have found that most people tend to excel at what they have an aptitude for. As an example, mathematicians usually choose that field because they have a talent for it and have been rewarded for that talent in the past. Similarly, car mechanics might choose their work not because they studied hard, but because early on they exhibited a mechanical talent. Thus, the admittedly unscientific test in Figure 2.2 just asks what you currently can do well. It assumes that if you can do something well, you have an aptitude for it. Doing badly on the test does not mean you have no aptitude or skill, just as doing well does not guarantee a skill or talent for a job.

As with the attitude test, there is no set number of correct answers that will guarantee success or failure. However, the more Yes answers you give, the better an indication that you have the skills, and probably the aptitude, to handle a successful job. A score of 17 or more in the Yes column is a definite indication that home remodeling could be for you; 14 to 17 indicates you'll probably like it; 13 and lower suggests that maybe you'd be better off trying your hand at an office job.

The Bottom Line

You must realize that no test can predict your success or failure at home remodeling. What these tests can do, however, is challenge you to ask yourself just how prepared you are for the tasks that lie ahead.

Chances are that if you're even considering home remodeling, you've had some background in building projects of one sort or another; you've therefore already been set in this direction. These two tests should merely be used to help you decide whether to continue on the path or to think about trying something else.

FIGURE 2.2 ■ Skills Test

	Yes	No
1. Are you healthy and can you handle moderate manual labor?	☐	☐
2. Do you keep abreast of the real estate market in your area?	☐	☐
3. Have you bought and sold a house before?	☐	☐
4. Can you look at a home and envision how to change walls, windows, doors and other features to make it more attractive and liveable?	☐	☐
5. Can you handle your own bookkeeping for tax purposes as well as for paying workpeople?	☐	☐
6. Do you have the funds available to buy a rehab home or other property and keep it vacant while you remodel it?	☐	☐
7. Do you have the time to do the work?	☐	☐
8. Do you understand basic real estate finance?	☐	☐
9. Do you work well with colors and patterns, as in paint and wallpaper?	☐	☐
10. Can you landscape a front yard?	☐	☐
11. Can you handle an electric drill?	☐	☐
12. What about a portable electric saw?	☐	☐
13. Can you hammer a nail in straight the first time?	☐	☐
14. Can you read a set of plans?	☐	☐
15. Can you create a set of plans from which others can work?	☐	☐
16. Do you understand basic home electrical circuits?	☐	☐
17. What about basic home plumbing?	☐	☐
18. Do you understand how a house is built: rafters, joists, walls, floors, roof and other components?	☐	☐
19. Have you ever added a wall or window or done other successful and extensive remodeling work?	☐	☐
20. Have you ever easily and successfully installed a garage-door opener?	☐	☐

CHAPTER 3

Estimating Costs

An important key to success in remodeling is getting an accurate estimate of what it will cost to repair and renovate the property. Underestimate the costs and you stand to lose money when it comes time to resell. Overestimate the costs and, if you're purchasing a property, you'll lose out on the purchase to someone with a sharper pencil. The goal is to be right on.

Unfortunately, accurate estimating takes experience, which is what you lack most when you first start. Nevertheless, even the first-timer can get a fairly accurate estimate just by being careful and by quickly checking with outside experts.

Another aid to precisely determining costs is one of the estimator books available in most bookstores. These list most of the renovation and building projects involved with rehabbing and give typical costs. Perhaps the best I've seen is *The Home Improvement Cost Guide* by the R. S. Means Company, Means Publishers, 1989. It gives both the cost of materials and the cost of having a builder do the work and is categorized according to different areas and even different cities in the country. The difficulty with this and similar books is that they tend not to really tell you what work you can do for yourself and what the materials will cost if you scout around and buy on sale. However, as noted, these books can be helpful as a starting point for the new remodeler.

■ ESTIMATING WORK TO BE DONE

Before you can determine costs, you must first determine accurately what work needs to be done. This can be far more difficult than it may seem at first. For example, you may be considering remodeling a kitchen. The cabinets seem old and dilapidated. Do they need to be replaced? If so, it could cost more than $5,000. On the other hand, can you get by with just repainting them and rehanging the cabinet doors? The cost here might be under $500.

Certainly, because of the cost differential, you're going to lean toward repainting rather than replacing. But some cabinets simply can't be easily fixed and repainted. They may have deteriorated too much. Furthermore, because the kitchen is such an important area of the home, when it comes time to resell, new cabinets may more than justify themselves with an increased sales price. So what do you do?

Once again, only experience can be your teacher. But a good rule of thumb is this: Kitchen refurbishing usually pays for itself dollar-for-dollar in resale price. The more you do for a kitchen (without going overboard and putting in solid-gold fixtures, of course), the more you'll get out of a property. My own inclination in the above example is that unless the cabinets can be fixed in such a way that they'll end up looking just like new, replace them. You'll be time and dollars ahead.

PRIORITIES OF REMODELING WORK

First, do work that returns more than it costs.

Second, do work that pays back dollar-for-dollar.

Third, only then consider work that returns less than it costs.

Your goal is to do work that returns more than it costs or at least pays back dollar-for-dollar. You want to avoid, whenever possible, work that returns less than it costs to do.

In later chapters we'll go into specific prices and times needed to complete many projects in the kitchen, bath and other areas of the house. In this chapter, we're going to be concerned with identifying problems and estimating time and costs.

You may want to copy the checklists in Figure 3.1 before using them so that they will be available for your use again. (As you get more experienced, you can add your own items to it.)

■ USING THE ESTIMATE CHECKLIST

Fill in your best estimate. When possible, get help from people in the field.

I've included a place under each heading where you can list the corrective work that needs to be done and estimate the time required and the cost. Even if you don't know the actual time and cost, fill in these blanks with your best guesses. This will help you to improve your estimating and will allow you to get a ballpark figure of total time and costs.

Also, sometimes rather than repair, you'll need to change or add to the existing area in order to improve the appearance or value of the house. In the checklists, I've indicated with an asterisk areas where this usually occurs.

FIGURE 3.1 ■ Buyer's Estimator

An evaluation checklist for determining the condition of a property and the time and cost involved in remodeling.

General

Property address: _____

Age: _____

Overall appearance: Good ___   Okay ___   Poor ___

Grading: Okay ___   Needs work ___

Drainage: Okay ___   Needs work ___

Cleanup (necessary before doing work—list items):

Yard: _____

_____

House: _____

_____

Yard

Driveway: Asphalt ___   Cement ___   Gravel ___   Other___

Condition: Good ___   Cracked ___   Holes ___   Not level ___

Work to be done: _____

_____

Time: _____ hrs.   Cost: $ _____

Walks: Cement ___   Stone ___   Stepping stones ___

Condition: Good ___   Cracked ___   Holes ___   Not level ___

Work to be done: _____

_____

Time: _____ hrs.   Cost: $ _____

Landscaping—Front: Complete ___   Partial ___   None ___

Condition: Good shape ___   Dead or dying ___   Needs trimming ___

FIGURE 3.1 *(continued)*

Lawn: Good ___   Needs water and trim ___   Needs revitalizing ___

   Needs trash removed ___

   Work to be done: _____

   _____

                                             Time: _____ hrs.   Cost: $ _____

Landscaping—Sides: Complete ___   Partial ___   None ___

   Condition: Good shape ___   Dead or dying ___   Needs trimming ___

Lawn: Good ___   Needs water and trim ___   Needs revitalizing ___

   Needs trash removed ___

   Work to be done: _____

   _____

                                             Time: _____ hrs.   Cost: $ _____

Landscaping—Back: Complete ___   Partial ___   None ___

   Condition: Good shape ___   Dead or dying ___   Needs trimming ___

Lawn: Good ___   Needs water and trim ___   Needs revitalizing ___

   Needs trash removed ___

   Work to be done: _____

   _____

                                             Time: _____ hrs.   Cost: $ _____

Drainage: Okay ___   Needs french drains, front ___   Left side ___

   Right side ___   Back ___

   Needs grading, front ___   Left side ___   Right side ___ Back ___

   Work to be done: _____

   _____

                                             Time: _____ hrs.   Cost: $ _____

FIGURE 3.1   *(continued)*

Fence: Good ___   Needs slats ___   Needs posts ___   Needs paint ___

   Needs straightening ___   Needs gate repair ___

   Needs new fence: Left side ___   Right side ___   Back ___   Front ___

   Work to be done: _____

   _____

                               Time: _____ hrs.   Cost: $ _____

Pool: Okay ___   Cracked ___   Tiles chipped ___   Pump not working ___

   Heater not working ___   Diving board needs repair ___

   Filter needs cleaning ___   Deck needs repair ___

   Work to be done: _____

   _____

                               Time: _____ hrs.   Cost: $ _____

House Exterior

Roof

   Type: Wood shingle ___   Cracked ___   Missing ___

   Wet or leaf-covered (indicating mold) ___

   Asphalt shingle ___   Curled ___   Missing ___   Discolored ___

   Tile ___   Cracked ___   Missing ___   Broken ___

   Tar & gravel ___   Patches ___   Other type ___

Ridges: Okay ___   Missing pieces ___

Valleys: Okay ___   Flashing rusted ___   Flashing broken ___

Gutters and downspouts: Okay ___   Broken ___   Missing ___

Overall roof condition: Good ___   Okay ___   Needs work ___   Leaks ___

   Work to be done: _____

   _____

                               Time: _____ hrs.   Cost: $ _____

FIGURE 3.1   *(continued)*

Walls

Type: Clapboard ___   Shingle ___   Brick ___   Stucco ___   Aluminum ___

    Stone ___   Vinyl ___   Other ___

    Condition: Okay ___   Cracking ___   Rotted ___   Dented ___

    Some missing ___ Crooked ___   Peeling ___   Loose ___

    Work to be done: _____

    _____

                                          Time: _____ hrs. Cost: $ _____

Paint or stain: Okay ___   Cracked and peeling ___   Faded ___   Discolored ___

    Work to be done: _____

    _____

                                          Time: _____ hrs. Cost: $ _____

Chimney: Okay ___   Cracked ___   Bricks missing ___

    Lightning arrestor missing ___   Spark arrestor missing ___   Mortar crumbling ___

    Work to be done: _____

    _____

                                          Time: _____ hrs. Cost: $ _____

Entrance: Okay ___   Cement cracked ___   Tiles cracked ___

    Wood floor sags and is weak ___

    * Should be changed to improve the appearance of house ___

    Work to be done: _____

    _____

                                          Time: _____ hrs. Cost: $ _____

Front door: Okay ___   Needs paint ___   Doesn't close properly ___

    * Should be changed to improve the appearance of house ___

    Work to be done: _____

    _____

                                          Time: _____ hrs. Cost: $ _____

FIGURE 3.1 *(continued)*

Back door: Okay ___   Needs paint ___   Doesn't close properly ___

   * Should be changed to improve the appearance of house ___

   Work to be done: _____

_____

                                Time: _____ hrs.   Cost: $ _____

House Interior

Entry

Ceiling: Okay ___   Discolored ___   Cracked ___   Peeling ___

   Water-stained ___   Needs paint ___   Needs to be reblown ___

Walls: Okay ___   Need wallpaper stripping ___   Need paint stripping ___

   Water-stained ___   Need new wallpaper or paint ___

   Need new electrical faceplates ___

Windows: Okay ___   Broken panes # ___   Need glazing # ___   Stuck ___

   Rot damage ___   Weather-stripped ___

Floors: Wood ___   Carpet ___   Ceramic tile ___   Marble ___   Slate ___

   Other tile ___   Linoleum ___   Buckled ___   Warped ___

   Water-stained ___   Holes ___   Gaps ___   Missing grout ___   Sag ___

   Noisy ___   Sloped ___

Stairway: Okay ___   Creaks ___   Steps broken ___

   Railing wobbles/damaged ___

Closet: Okay ___   Door missing ___   Door won't close ___

   Door damaged ___   Interior needs paint ___   Interior needs work ___

   Work to be done: _____

_____

                                Time: _____ hrs.   Cost: $ _____

FIGURE 3.1 *(continued)*

Kitchen

Ceiling: Okay ___ Discolored ___ Cracked ___ Peeling ___

   Water-stained ___ Needs paint ___ Needs to be reblown ___

Walls: Okay ___ Need wallpaper stripping ___ Need paint stripping ___

   Water-stained ___ Need new wallpaper or paint ___

   Need new electrical faceplates ___ Need GFI (Ground Fault Interrupter) plugs ___

Windows: Okay ___ Broken panes # ___ Need glazing # ___ Stuck ___

   Rot damage ___ Weather-protected ___

Floors: Wood ___ Carpet ___ Linoleum ___ Ceramic tile ___ Marble ___

   Slate ___ Other tile ___ Buckled ___ Warped ___ Water-stained ___

   Holes ___ Gaps ___ Missing grout ___ Sag ___ Noisy ___ Sloped ___

Cabinets: Okay ___ Stained ___ Doors don't fit ___ Old-fashioned ___

   Not enough ___ Hardware broken or mismatched ___

   * Should be changed to improve appearance of house ___

Counters: Ceramic ___ Formica ___ Wood ___ Other ___ Cracked ___

   Burnt ___ Stained ___ Other damage ___

   * Should be changed to improve appearance of house ___

Sink: Okay ___ Broken ___ Cracked ___ Stained ___ Other damage ___

   Drain discolored or damaged ___ Ugly ___ Faucets leaking ___

   Faucets ugly ___ Water flow insufficient ___

   * Should be changed to improve appearance of house ___

Garbage disposal: Okay ___ Missing ___ Inoperative ___

   * Should be changed to improve salability of house ___

Dishwasher: Okay ___ Missing ___ Inoperative ___ Looks old-fashioned ___

   Rusted or stained inside ___

   * Should be changed to improve salability of house ___

FIGURE 3.1 *(continued)*

Light fixtures: Okay ___   Broken ___   Incandescent ___   Fluorescent ___
Inadequate ___
* Should be changed to improve salability of house ___

Stove/Oven: Gas ___   Electric ___   Okay ___   Missing ___   Old-fashioned ___
Stained/discolored ___   Inoperative ___   Exhaust fan broken ___
* Should be added to improve salability of house ___

Work to be done: _____

_____

Time: _____ hrs. Cost: $ _____

Bath 1

Ceiling: Okay ___   Discolored ___   Cracked ___   Peeling ___
Water-stained ___   Needs paint ___   Needs to be reblown ___

Walls: Okay ___   Need wallpaper stripping ___   Need paint stripping ___
Water-stained ___   Need new wallpaper or paint ___   Need new electrical
faceplates ___   Need GFI (Ground Fault Interrupter) plugs ___

Windows: Okay ___   Broken panes # ___   Need glazing # ___   Stuck ___
Rot damage ___   Weather-protected ___

Floors: Wood ___   Carpet ___   Linoleum ___   Ceramic tile ___   Marble ___
Slate ___   Other tile ___   Buckled ___   Warped ___   Water-stained ___
Holes ___   Gaps ___   Missing grout ___   Sag ___   Noisy ___   Sloped ___

Cabinets: Okay ___   Stained ___   Doors don't fit ___   Old-fashioned ___
Not enough ___   Hardware broken or mismatched ___
* Should be changed to improve appearance of house ___

Counters: Ceramic ___   Formica ___   Wood ___   Other ___   Cracked ___
Burnt ___   Stained ___   Other damage ___
* Should be changed to improve appearance of house ___

FIGURE 3.1   *(continued)*

Sink: Okay ___   Broken ___   Cracked ___   Stained ___   Other damage ___

    Drain discolored or damaged ___   Ugly ___   Faucets leaking ___

    Faucets ugly ___   Water flow insufficient ___

    * Should be changed to improve appearance of house ___

Shower/Tub: Fiberglass ___   Tile ___   Other ___   Okay ___   Broken ___

    Cracked ___   Stained ___   Other damage ___

    Drain discolored or damaged ___ Leaking ___   Faucets ugly ___

    Water flow insufficient ___

    * Should be changed to improve appearance of house ___

    Work to be done: _____

    _____

                              Time: _____ hrs.   Cost: $ _____

Bath 2

Ceiling: Okay ___   Discolored ___   Cracked ___   Peeling ___

    Water-stained ___   Needs paint ___   Needs to be reblown ___

Walls: Okay ___   Need wallpaper stripping ___   Need paint stripping ___

    Water-stained ___   Need new wallpaper or paint ___   Need new electrical

    faceplates ___   Need GFI (Ground Fault Interrupter) plugs ___

Windows: Okay ___ Broken panes # ___   Need glazing # ___   Stuck ___

    Rot damage ___   Weather-stripped ___

Floors: Wood ___   Carpet ___   Linoleum ___   Ceramic tile ___   Marble ___

    Slate ___   Other tile ___   Buckled ___   Warped ___   Water-stained ___

    Holes ___   Gaps ___   Missing grout ___   Sag ___   Noisy ___   Sloped ___

Cabinets: Okay ___ Stained ___   Doors don't fit ___   Old-fashioned ___

    Not enough ___   Hardware broken or mismatched ___

    * Should be changed to improve appearance of house ___

FIGURE 3.1   *(continued)*

Counters: Ceramic ___   Formica ___   Wood ___   Other ___   Cracked ___

   Burnt ___   Stained ___   Other damage ___

   * Should be changed to improve appearance of house ___   .

Sink: Okay ___   Broken ___   Cracked ___   Stained ___   Other damage ___

   Drain discolored or damaged ___   Ugly ___   Faucets leaking ___

   Faucets ugly ___   Water flow insufficient ___

   * Should be changed to improve appearance of house ___

Shower/Tub: Fiberglass ___   Tile ___   Other ___   Okay ___   Broken ___

   Cracked ___   Stained ___   Other damage ___

   Drain discolored or damaged ___   Leaking ___   Faucets ___   Ugly ___

   Water flow insufficient ___

   * Should be changed to improve appearance of house ___

   Work to be done: _____

   _____

                             Time: _____ hrs.   Cost: $ _____

Living room

   Too small

   * Should be changed to improve appearance of house ___

Ceiling: Okay ___   Discolored ___   Cracked ___   Peeling ___

   Water-stained ___   Needs paint ___   Needs to be reblown ___

Walls: Okay ___   Need wallpaper stripping ___   Need paint stripping ___

   Water-stained ___   Need new wallpaper or paint ___   Need new electrical

   faceplates ___

Fireplace: Stone ___   Brick ___   Other ___   Damper works ___

   Damper missing ___   Discolored ___   Broken ___   Mantel level ___

   Smoke damage ___

FIGURE 3.1 *(continued)*

Windows: Okay ___ Broken panes # ___ Need glazing # ___ Stuck ___
   Rot damage ___ Weather-stripped ___

Floors: Wood ___ Carpet ___ Linoleum ___ Ceramic tile ___ Marble ___
   Slate ___ Other tile ___ Buckled ___ Warped ___ Water-stained ___
   Holes ___ Gaps ___ Missing grout ___ Sag ___ Noisy ___ Sloped ___

Stairway: Okay ___ Creaks ___ Steps broken ___
   Railing wobbles/damaged ___

Closet: Okay ___ Door missing ___ Door won't close ___
   Door damaged ___ Interior needs paint ___ Interior needs work ___
   Work to be done: _____

_____

                                        Time: _____ hrs. Cost: $ _____

Dining room

Ceiling: Okay ___ Discolored ___ Cracked ___ Peeling ___
   Water-stained ___ Needs paint ___ Needs to be reblown ___

Light fixture: Okay ___ Missing ___ Ugly ___
   * Should be changed to improve appearance of house ___

Walls: Okay ___ Need wallpaper stripping ___ Need paint stripping ___
   Water-stained ___ Need new wallpaper or paint ___ Need new electrical
   faceplates ___

Windows: Okay ___ Broken panes # ___ Need glazing # ___ Stuck ___
   Rot damage ___ Weather-stripped ___

Floors: Wood ___ Carpet ___ Linoleum ___ Ceramic tile ___ Marble ___
   Slate ___ Other tile ___ Buckled ___ Warped ___ Water-stained ___
   Holes ___ Gaps ___ Missing grout ___ Sag ___ Noisy ___ Sloped ___

Stairway: Okay ___ Creaks ___ Steps broken ___
   Railing wobbles/damaged ___

FIGURE 3.1 *(continued)*

Closet: Okay ___   Door missing ___   Door won't close ___   Door damaged ___
Interior needs paint ___   Interior needs work ___
Work to be done: _____

_____

Time: _____ hrs.   Cost: $ _____

Family room

First floor ___   In basement ___   Recreation room ___   Too small ___
* Should be changed to improve appearance of house ___

Ceiling: Okay ___   Discolored ___   Cracked ___   Peeling ___
Water-stained ___   Needs paint ___   Needs to be reblown ___

Walls: Okay ___   Need wallpaper stripping ___   Need paint stripping ___
Water-stained ___   Need new wallpaper or paint ___   Need new electrical
faceplates ___

Fireplace: Stone ___   Brick ___   Other ___   Damper works ___
Damper missing ___   Discolored ___   Broken ___   Mantel level ___
Smoke damage ___

Windows: Okay ___   Broken panes # ___   Need glazing # ___   Stuck ___
Rot damage ___   Weather-stripped ___

Floors: Wood ___   Carpet ___   Linoleum ___   Ceramic tile ___   Marble ___
Slate ___   Other tile ___   Buckled ___   Warped ___   Water-stained ___
Holes ___   Gaps ___   Missing grout ___   Sag ___   Noisy ___   Sloped ___

Stairway: Okay ___   Creaks ___   Steps broken ___
Railing wobbles/damaged ___

Closet: Okay ___   Door missing ___   Door won't close ___   Door damaged ___
Interior needs paint ___   Interior needs work ___
Work to be done: _____

_____

Time: _____ hrs.   Cost: $ _____

FIGURE 3.1 *(continued)*

Master bedroom

Separated from rest of house ___   Has attached bathroom ___

   * Bath should be added to improve salability of house ___

Ceiling: Okay ___   Discolored ___   Cracked ___   Peeling ___

   Water-stained ___   Needs paint ___   Needs to be reblown ___

Walls: Okay ___   Need wallpaper stripping ___   Need paint stripping ___

   Water-stained ___   Need new wallpaper or paint ___   Need new electrical

   faceplates ___

Windows: Okay ___   Broken panes # ___   Need glazing # ___   Stuck ___

   Rot damage ___   Weather-stripped ___

Floors: Wood ___   Carpet ___   Linoleum ___   Ceramic tile ___   Marble ___

   Slate ___   Other tile ___   Buckled ___   Warped ___   Water-stained ___

   Holes ___   Gaps ___   Missing grout ___   Sag ___   Noisy ___   Sloped ___

Stairway: Okay ___   Creaks ___   Steps broken ___

   Railing wobbles/damaged ___

Closet: Okay ___   Door missing ___   Door won't close ___   Door damaged ___

   Interior needs paint ___   Interior needs work ___

   Work to be done: _____

   _____

                                          Time: _____ hrs. Cost: $ _____

Bedroom 2

Ceiling: Okay ___   Discolored ___   Cracked ___   Peeling ___

   Water-stained ___   Needs paint ___   Needs to be reblown ___

Walls: Okay ___   Need wallpaper stripping ___   Need paint stripping ___

   Water-stained ___   Need new wallpaper or paint ___   Need new electrical

   faceplates ___   Need GFI (Ground Fault Interrupter) plugs ___

FIGURE 3.1   *(continued)*

Windows: Okay ___   Broken panes # ___   Need glazing # ___   Stuck ___

Rot damage ___   Weather-stripped ___

Floors: Wood ___   Carpet ___   Linoleum ___   Ceramic tile ___   Marble ___

Slate ___   Other tile ___   Buckled ___   Warped ___   Water-stained ___

Holes ___   Gaps ___   Missing grout ___   Sag ___   Noisy ___   Sloped ___

Closet: Okay ___   Door missing ___   Door won't close ___   Door damaged ___

Interior needs paint ___   Interior needs work ___

Work to be done: _____

_____

Time: _____ hrs.   Cost: $ _____

Bedroom 3

Ceiling: Okay ___   Discolored ___   Cracked ___   Peeling ___

Water-stained ___   Needs paint ___   Needs to be reblown ___

Walls: Okay ___   Need wallpaper stripping ___   Need paint stripping ___

Water-stained ___   Need new wallpaper or paint ___   Need new electrical

face plates ___   Need GFI (Ground Fault Interrupter) plugs ___

Windows: Okay ___   Broken panes # ___   Need glazing # ___   Stuck ___

Rot damage ___   Weather-stripped ___

Floors: Wood ___   Carpet ___   Linoleum ___   Ceramic tile ___   Marble ___

Slate ___   Other tile ___   Buckled ___   Warped ___   Water-stained ___

Holes ___   Gaps ___   Missing grout ___   Sag ___   Noisy ___   Sloped ___

Closet: Okay ___   Door missing ___   Door won't close ___   Door damaged ___

Interior needs paint ___   Interior needs work ___

Work to be done: _____

_____

Time: _____ hrs.   Cost: $ _____

FIGURE 3.1   *(continued)*

Attic: Leaks ___   Insulation ___   Broken/sagging beams ___

  Garbage needs clean-up ___   Properly vented ___

  Work to be done: _____

  _____

                                        Time: _____ hrs.   Cost: $ _____

Basement: Finished ___   Unfinished ___   Washer/dryer space ___

Lights: Adequate ___   None ___

Stairs: Okay ___   Too steep ___   Broken ___

Floor: Concrete ___   Dirt ___   Wood ___   Other ___   Standing water ___

  Water stains ___   Rot/mold ___   Garbage needing clean-up ___

Walls: Cement ___   Cement blocks ___   Wood ___   Brick ___   Other ___

  Damp ___   Insulated ___   Cracked ___   Holes ___

Ceiling: Too low ___   Sagging beams ___

  Work to be done: _____

  _____

                                        Time: _____ hrs.   Cost: $ _____

Garage: Yes ___   Carport only ___   Storage ___   Washer/dryer ___   Space ___

  Finished ___   Unfinished ___

Lights: Adequate ___   None ___

Floor: Concrete ___   Dirt ___   Other ___   Garbage needing clean-up ___

Walls: Cement ___   Cement blocks ___   Wood ___   Brick ___   Other ___

  Cracked ___   Holes ___

                                        Time: _____ hrs.   Cost: $ _____

Electrical system: Insufficient outlets ___   Which rooms? ___

  Main disconnect ___   Circuit breakers ___   Fuses ___   Amps # ___

  Insufficient power ___   Wiring inadequate ___

FIGURE 3.1   *(continued)*

Rewiring needed in which rooms? _____

Work to be done: _____

_____

Time: _____ hrs. Cost: $ _____

Heating system: Central ___   Perimeter ___   Too old ___   Gas ___   Electric ___

Oil ___   Coal ___   Solar ___   Steam ___   Hot water ___

Forced air ___   Gravity feed ___   BTUs ___   Insufficient BTUs ___

Heating ducts to each room ___   Ducts rusted or damaged ___

Combustion chamber: Clean ___   Cracked ___

Electric control switch: Okay ___   None ___   Inoperative ___

* Should be added to improve salability of house ___

Work to be done: _____

_____

Time: _____ hrs. Cost: $ _____

Plumbing system: Copper ___   Galvanized ___

Shut-off valves outside and inside ___   Leaks—where? _____

Rusty joints (indicating future leaks) ___   Sewer cleanouts ___   Sewer ___

Septic ___   Drain problems—where? _____

Water heater age ___   Makes rumbling noises ___   Rusty ___   Leaks ___

Safety relief valve not installed ___   Vent not open or missing __

Gas supply pipe inadequate ___

Work to be done: _____

_____

Time: _____ hrs. Cost: $ _____

Smoke alarms: Cover all areas ___   Missing ___

FIGURE 3.1   *(continued)*

Work to be done: _____

_____

Time: _____ hrs.   Cost: $ _____

Security system: None ____   Installed ____   Not working ____

Work to be done: _____

_____

Time: _____ hrs.   Cost: $ _____

Total time: _____

Total cost: _____

CHAPTER 4

Judging How Much To Do

There is the old story of the man who bought a fishing boat. All his life he wanted to spend some time fishing. Now that he was retired and had a few dollars, he was going to realize a lifelong dream.

However, he couldn't afford a new boat, so he bought an old one. He spent months fixing it up. He had the engine rebuilt, put in a new galley and had the old teak decks refinished. He put in countless hours staining and painting and cleaning.

Finally, one bright morning his boat was ready. Armed with fishing gear and bait he proudly sailed out to sea.

Unfortunately, this story has a sad ending. Just a few miles from the harbor, his boat sprang a leak and sank. The would-be fisherman was never seen again.

It turned out that of all the dozens of things he had done to the boat, the one thing that he had not done was to check and fix the hull. It was only one thing of many, but it was one of the most important, and he had overlooked it. Much the same holds true with remodeling. There are dozens and dozens of different things you may need to do to shape up your house. Chances are that only a few of these are critical. If you are going to be able to resell for a profit (or at least the money you put in), you don't want to miss any of the critical items that could sink your project.

In this chapter we're going to look at what it pays to do and what it doesn't pay to do. In short, we're going to judge which work makes sense for you to spend your time on. Along the way we'll consider the other side of the coin, doing so much that you overremodel.

■ WHAT ADDS VALUE

Some things that you can do to a property that will add value are obvious. You can paint the front. You can get rid of any garbage and trash lying around. If there's anything broken, like windows, or holes in walls, you can fix them. You don't need this book or any other to tell you to do these things, but beyond, the whole area of remodeling gets fuzzy. Should you modernize the kitchen and bath? What about tearing out the wall between the living room and dining room? Should you add a deck?

How can you determine which additional projects will add to the value of the property and which are just wasted time and money? You can check into the charts at the end of this chapter. When you do, consider a method I have found useful for determining which remodeling job to do, called the detracting factor.

■ THE DETRACTING FACTOR

Most houses that are suitable for remodeling have at least one big detracting factor. This is the feature of the house that most makes it need remodeling. Find this feature, correct it, and you've dramatically improved the property. If all goes well, you can now (if you so desire) resell the property for a whopping profit.

Your goal is to find that detracting factor. Once you've done so, you must accurately determine whether it can be fixed and, if so, how much it will cost. This calculation will go a long way toward determining whether the property can be profitable.

Beware of problems that are too obvious. Yes, the kitchen is a wreck and needs to be remodeled, but is the real problem the fact that the house is badly located? If so, nothing will save it and you're wasting time attempting to remodel.

Yes, it's obvious the bathroom needs new fixtures, but is the real problem that the foundation is cracked and the house is leaning to one side? No matter how well you fix up the bath, a leaning house is unsalable and your remodeling efforts will be for naught.

Yes, the walls need repainting and repapering and the floor needs to be recarpeted (or restained), but is the house so old that the rooms are simply too small for a modern family? No matter how nice you make them, would you be better off knocking down a few walls and turning two tiny rooms into one big one?

Find the detracting factor, the one thing that really makes a big difference, and do that first. If you don't, you're simply wasting valuable time and money.

RULES FOR FINDING THE DETRACTING FACTORS

1. Identify the detracting factor before deciding to move ahead.

2. Determine how much it will cost to remedy.

3. Never forget, overlook, discount or avoid dealing with the detracting factor.

■ THE WHITE ELEPHANT SYNDROME

Someday you will want to sell the house you remodel. That is almost a certainty. But will you be able to sell for what you've put in?

One of the hardest properties to resell is one that is overbuilt for the neighborhood. Take a run-down neighborhood where every house needs repair and then remodel just one of them. What you end up with is a pearl in a bed of mud. Prospective buyers, if you can find any, might give a few thousand dollars extra for the improvements you've made.

Generally they'll offer close to what the other still run-down houses are selling for. In short, you'll never get out the money you put in.

The problem comes from putting your own standards ahead of common sense. Isn't there a kind of home that you would really like to have, an ideal house? It may have plush carpeting, large spacious rooms and superfluous amenities such as towel warmers in the bathroom. It's what you would really like to have if you could design and build your own home without thought of reselling. When you remodel, that's sort of what you do. You redesign and rebuild. Along the way you can add all the wonderful things you always wanted in a house if you're not careful.

If you let your desires take charge, you could end up spending so much money remodeling a property that you could never sell it for what you've put in. It could become a white elephant.

The Big White House

This is a true story. A couple of friends of mine decided that they wanted to remodel their existing home. They had bought the house some ten years earlier and hadn't done ten cents' worth of work on it in that time. It needed everything from carpets to paint, from window coverings to a new stove and oven.

Of course, they tried to be practical. They figured, correctly, that if they sold their home as is, they would get far less than if they remodeled the place and sold it for top dollar. However, selling was not their intention at the time. In fact, they dreamt that they would live there forever.

As a result, they didn't bother to work up a budget and a list of items that were suitable for remodeling. Instead, they knew what they wanted the place to look like, so they went forward spending and began fixing in a frenzy of activity.

The house was single story, but quite spread out. They painted all the walls and trim. They ordered expensive wallpaper and the best-quality carpeting. They paid a fortune for an Italian marble entryway. They ripped out the kitchen, although the cabinets were perfectly acceptable, and put in all new stained oak units. A top-of-the-line self-cleaning stove/oven with built-in microwave was also added.

While they were buying cabinets for the kitchen, they ordered a whole series of cabinets for the living room and, deciding that the detracting factor was that there wasn't enough room, they hired a contractor to come over and knock out one wall by the living room. Then they added a 300-square-foot family room with vaulted beam ceilings and a fireplace.

Of course, the house had to have all new fixtures, including gold door handles and expensive hanging lamps inside and out. They had the place totally landscaped and added a spa.

When it was finished they invited my wife and me over. Naturally, we oohed and aahed when we were supposed to. In reality, it really wasn't hard to give them credit. They had truly done a wonderful job. The house was worthy of Beverly Hills.

The problem was that it wasn't located in Beverly Hills. It was located amid other tract homes, none of which were even remotely as plush.

A year later, their circumstances changed. She lost her job and he had to take a pay cut in his. They decided to move out of the state and sell their home. However, when they added up all their costs (they had meticulously kept track of all remodeling purchases) they found that just to break even, they had to sell for $350,000. That amount just included their purchase cost and their remodeling costs.

The trouble was that the most any house in the neighborhood had ever sold for was $300,000. They were almost $50,000 high for the neighborhood. Adding in a profit, they hoped to sell for $390,000.

They tried and tried. Needless to say, there simply weren't any buyers at their price. The oldest rule in real estate prevailed: Location, location and location are the three most important factors in determining price.

Buyers who could afford to pay $390,000 wanted a $390,000 neighborhood, in part so they wouldn't have trouble reselling. Eventually, it became clear to my friends that in order to sell, they were going to have to lower their price closer to the $300,000 mark. They were going to have to sell at a loss!

Ultimately, they decided not to sell. This story has a happy ending because they liked what they had done so much that they decided to keep making payments on the big mortgage (required to pay for the work) and live there indefinitely, or until inflation eventually boosted the value of surrounding houses to a level at which they could at least sell for their costs. As of this writing, they are still there, nearly seven years later.

The real trouble was that they broke a cardinal rule of remodeling. Never overimprove. Never put more money into the property than you can reasonably expect to get out.

■ THE RENAISSANCE EXPERIENCE

An exception to the overimprovement rule can be seen in a neighborhood going through a renaissance. In some Victorian and old brownstone sections of city centers, many enterprising rehabbers are moving into run-down neighborhoods and revitalizing them. On any given block you may see half a dozen houses in the process of renovation. This entire-neighborhood home remodeling presents a real opportunity. You can often buy the older homes for a song, remodel them and, once the neighborhood turns, sell for a big profit.

The key is timing. You don't want to buy before there is a clear indication that the entire neighborhood is undergoing renovation. On the other hand, if you wait too long, the prices of the remaining run-down houses will soar as their owners seek to cash in on the turnaround. I apply the 30/70 rule here.

If 30 percent of the neighborhood has been rehabilitated within the last two years, nothing will likely stop the remaining 70 percent from going along.

■ THE PERFECT LOCATION FOR REMODELING

The perfect location for a property to remodel (whether you're in it now or going to buy) is in an upscale section of town. Ideally all the homes will be well kept and the neighborhood will have a prestigious quality to it. In short, there will be demand for the homes in any kind of market.

What you want is the decrepit house. You want the bad apple in the barrel of good fruit (not a good apple in a barrel of moldy fruit). You want to remodel a home that's dilapidated, run-down in a great area of town. Is this a description of your property?

■ TAKE TIME TO REFLECT

After you've checked out the charts at the end of the chapter to see how much financial sense your prospective remodeling job makes, take a few minutes to sit down in the house with no one else around (preferably in the room where you're going to do the work) and get the feel of it. Does it feel right? Or is there something wrong that you might have overlooked?

This moment of reflection before making a decision is the best few minutes you can spend. Often, on reflection, you realize that something just doesn't add up—that there's another major problem involved in the home that you haven't touched on. Maybe it's the location. Perhaps it's a detracting feature. But something just isn't right.

Now it's time to go searching again. Armed with your suspicions that you've left something out, you probably have a better chance of identifying what's really wrong.

RULES FOR JUDGING HOW MUCH WORK TO DO

- ■ Never add features that the neighboring houses don't have.

- ■ Don't add on until you've identified the major detracting feature.

- ■ Remodel according to the neighborhood, not according to your dreams.

- ■ Always consider the value added by the remodeling job you are considering.

Ultimately, of course, it's a judgment call. However, to help you make that judgment, here are some clues. Generally speaking, you should do only work that will return dollar-for-dollar what you spend. For example, if you put in carpeting for $3,000, you want the property to increase in value and sell for $3,000 more than it would without the new carpeting, at minimum.

Ideally, you want the return to be greater than dollar-for-dollar; otherwise you wouldn't be in the business of rehabbing. For example, new carpeting that costs $3,000 may actually make the property so attractive that it will sell for $10,000 more. That's the ideal.

Judging the return you'll get from a particular remodeling job is difficult because each property is different and because sometimes you have to spend money with no apparent return, as when you need to retrofit the electrical system. No buyer is going to pay extra for a retrofitted electrical system because there's no visible evidence of the work done. On the other hand, most buyers won't purchase unless the electrical system works well and is modernized.

To put it another way, fixing the electrical system may be money you'll have to spend just to be able to sell at any price. Other similar items are the plumbing and heating systems of the home. No one will buy a house for top dollar if the plumbing doesn't work or there isn't any heat.

We're not going to consider these invisible-cost items in this chapter. Rather, we're going to consider what visible items you can spend your money on and how much of a return you can expect.

In all cases the maximum return we'll consider is 200 percent. That means that the improvement adds twice what it cost to the property. Of course, it might add much more than that, but that's more a factor of the individual property than the improvement.

On the other hand, the return might be significantly less depending on how well you do the job, the expectations for the neighborhood, the quality of materials and the economic conditions at the time. Keep in mind that the following chart is really just an estimate based on my 30 years of experience. No guarantees can be given!

In Figure 4.1, the areas that will give the best return on cost are listed first and those with the least return on cost are listed last.

FIGURE 4.1 ■ Maximum Possible Return on Cost

Landscaping Front—Overall	**200 %**
Green, full lawns	200 %
In-season flowers (colorful)	200 %
Potted plants (lush, green)	200 %
Remove rubbish, trash	200 %
Clean and trim	200 %
Add hedges (trimmed)	100 %
New stepping stones	100 %
Add trees (trimmed)	50 %
Add sprinklers	50 %
New cement path	50 %
Entryway—Overall	**200 %**
New front doors (hardwood)	200 %
New tile/wood entry	200 %
Outside deck entrance	200 %
New wall covering (paint, wallpaper)	150 %
New light fixture	150 %
Kitchen—Overall	**200 %**
New countertops/sink	200 %
New floor (wood, tile, linoleum)	200 %
New wall covering (paint, wallpaper)	200 %
New cabinet doors	150 %
Add garbage disposal/dishwasher	150 %
New light fixtures	100 %
New stove/oven	100 %

FIGURE 4.1   *(continued)*

Refinished cabinets and doors	100 %
New cabinets	70 %
Replace dishwasher	50 %
Replace garbage disposal	25 %
Driveway Front—Overall	**150 %**
New cement/asphalt drive	150 %
New gravel	100 %
New curb	75 %
Main Bath—Overall	**150 %**
New tub/shower	150 %
New sliding glass doors on tub/shower	150 %
New flooring	150 %
New sink/cabinet	150 %
New paint/wallpaper	150 %
New sink	100 %
New medicine cabinet	100 %
New toilet	75 %
New racks, handles, etc.	50 %
Add other fixtures (towel warmer)	25 %
Living/Dining/Family Room/Rumpus Room—Overall	**100 %**
New flooring (wood, carpet)	100 %
New wall covering (paint, wallpaper)	100 %
Reblow acoustical ceiling	100 %
New fixtures	50 %

FIGURE 4.1 *(continued)*

Resurface fireplace	50 %
Window seats	50 %
Master Bedroom—Overall	**100 %**
Add master bath	100 %
New flooring (wood, carpet)	100 %
New wall covering (paint, wallpaper)	100 %
New fixtures	50 %
Resurface fireplace	50 %
Window seats	50 %
Bath—Overall	**100 %**
New tub/shower	100 %
New sliding glass doors on tub/shower	100 %
New flooring	100 %
New sink/cabinet	100 %
New paint/wallpaper	100 %
New sink	75 %
New medicine cabinet	75 %
New toilet	50 %
New racks, handles, etc.	25 %
Add other fixtures (towel warmer)	25 %
Other Bedrooms—Overall	**75 %**
New flooring (wood, carpet)	75 %
New wall covering (paint, wallpaper)	75 %
New fixtures	50 %

FIGURE 4.1   *(continued)*

Resurface fireplace	50 %
Window seats	25 %
Basement—Overall	**50 %**
New flooring	50 %
New wall covering (paint, wallpaper)	25 %
New insulation	25 %
Landscaping Backyard—Overall	**50 %**
Deck	50 %
Green, full lawns	50 %
In-season flowers (colorful)	50 %
Potted plants (lush, green)	50 %
Remove rubbish, trash	50 %
Clean and trim	50 %
Add hedges (trimmed)	35 %
New stepping stones	35 %
Add trees (trimmed)	35 %
Add sprinklers	35 %
New cement path	25 %
Attic—Overall	**50 %**
New insulation	50–100 %
New lighting	10 %
***Add-Ons—Overall**	**50 %**
Room	50 %
Window (with seat, box)	50 %

FIGURE 4.1 *(continued)*

Skylight	50 %
Doorway	50 %
Exterior	100 %
New paint	200 %
Storm windows	100 %
Aluminum siding	50 %
Security system	50 %
Screens	50 %
Re-stucco	25 %

* I consider add-ons optional. However, when they correct a major detracting factor, they are necessary and return far more than they cost.

■ ═ CHAPTER 5 ═ ■

Doing It Yourself or Paying Others

Everyone I know wants to save money. In fact, I've never met anyone who wanted to waste money. As a result, when it comes to remodeling, all of us do our best to cut costs. One of the easiest and quickest ways to cut costs, as most of us perceive it, is to do the work ourselves.

A door doesn't fit right. We'll take it off its hinges, shave a bit off the top, and it'll be perfect. Or a countertop looks bad, so we'll buy new tile and lay it. A floor sags, so we'll go underneath and jack it up and brace it. Or the outside stucco is cracking and peeling, so we'll replaster. The list of items we see ourselves doing can be endless. Indeed, if we're industrious, know how to do the work and have the time, there really isn't a single remodeling job that we can't do ourselves, or with a little help from a friend.

The real questions are the following:

- Can we learn, or is it a skill that requires training?

- Do we know how to do the work?

- Do we have the time?

- Does it pay for us to do it?

The immediate answer most remodelers give is that no matter what, they'll do it themselves, at least at first. Only if they find that they can't do it will they hire a professional.

My goal in this chapter is to convince those of you who feel this way that probably half of the time you are wrong! Many times it pays to have someone else who is more knowledgeable, trained and skillful do the work. It can save you time and money to have the expert do it.

I must confess that I also have a personal motive for this desire to convince. I am the worst culprit when it comes to fixing things. I always want to do everything myself and it's only after bitter lessons learned over the years (as well as pointed arguments from my wife) that I have learned to hire others to do certain work. I hope you will benefit from my experience.

■ DOES A PRO REALLY COST MORE?

When we're remodeling, as I noted above, we want to save money because the budget is usually tight. Every dollar we avoid spending is another dollar in our pockets. The question I pose here is whether hiring a professional to do a job really costs more than doing it ourselves. To understand my reasoning here, let's consider what I call the rule of the single project. First, we'll apply it to buying building materials, then we'll examine it with regard to labor.

■ MATERIALS AND THE SINGLE-PROJECT RULE

This is probably the most misunderstood principle of remodeling (and many other things as well). It is most commonly misused in books on remodeling and similar subjects that purport to tell you how much it costs to do something.

The rule of the single project works like this. Some people assume that when they need to buy something, they'll pay top dollar because they need to buy only one. You need a bathtub, so you go to the hardware store and buy one for close to full retail.

On the other hand, some people assume that there are economies involved with buying multiple items. Let's say that you're a builder and you need to buy ten medicine cabinets for homes you are building. Where are you going to buy them and how much are you going to pay?

You could go to the same hardware store and buy them, paying close to retail. If you did that, you'd be a foolish builder because you could go to a building-supply store and, using your builder's discount, get them at a price closer to wholesale. In short, because you are buying ten instead of only one, you should be able to get a better price.

This reasoning leads most remodelers to conclude that because we can't buy in quantity, we must pay more. (Note: Some remodelers feel that if they get a contractor's license, they can buy for less. I don't use a contractor's license, but have worked with many people who do. I find that the discount to contractors is often offset by the fact that they have to buy at a store that usually charges more. Thus, the savings are often illusory.)

The truth, however, is in the Rule of the Single Project: When we need to make only a single purchase, we are not at a disadvantage. Rather, we are in a better position. The reason is that we can take advantage of closeouts, remainders and special sales.

The Rule of the Single Project says that when you need to buy only one of an item, you can often get it for a fraction of its retail cost if you look carefully.

Recently, I had to buy a medicine cabinet for a bathroom remodeling job I was doing. I went to the local discount building-supply store. The cabinets I liked cost around $150. (I was buying an oak unit.) However, they had one left of a discontinued model with a scratch on one side. They were willing to sell it for $50. I purchased it, put a little stain on the scratch (which made the defect invisible) and used it.

Because I had to buy only one, I was able to take advantage of savings that would not have been available if I had to buy ten. I'm quite

sure that a builder who needed to buy ten, even at the deepest discount, would have had to pay significantly more per cabinet than the
$50 I paid.

■ LABOR AND THE SINGLE-PROJECT RULE

The same principle holds true for labor. When a builder hires
labor, he or she must deal with subcontractors, unions and pay scales.
On the other hand, when you hire labor for your small job, you usually can deal with an individual worker, often one who is doing the
job on his or her own time.

For example, I recently needed to have a water heater moved from
a kitchen area to a porch. The job involved not only moving the heavy
heater, but also retrofitting the plumbing to lead out and join the
heater on the porch.

If I had found a plumbing company in the phone book and called,
I am quite sure that the job would have cost $500 to $1,000. However,
I've made friends with many people in the building trades. I knew a
plumber who was looking for some extra work on his own and called
him. He said he'd do it for $100 plus parts.

Was it worth my time to disconnect and lug a heavy heater across
the house, then crawl underneath and work with old pipe, perhaps
breaking it, trying to reroute the plumbing, when I could hire a pro to
do it for $100? I hired him on the spot.

Note: We're asking a professional such as a plumber or an electrician to bid on a job. He or she can bid any price and you can accept or
reject the offer. However, professionals who work on their own time
to make a little extra money will often do it for less. This usually only
works, however, because you have a small, single project to do. That's
the Rule of the Single Project.

■ HOW TO FIND WORKPEOPLE

You can use the phone book. However, as soon as you begin
remodeling, you'll run into a couple of workpeople who will see you

as a source of a few extra bucks now and then. They'll tell you about friends of theirs. Eventually, you'll build a network.

I can't imagine remodeling for six months and not knowing a dozen people in different building professions whom I could call upon. The very nature of the single-project work we are doing lends itself to these sorts of networks.

The point is that once you understand and accept the single-project rule, you come to realize that it doesn't cost as much as you may think to have someone else do the work. In fact, it may cost far less than you dare guess!

■ WHAT WOULD IT COST YOU TO DO THE WORK?

On the other hand, when you do the work, it isn't free. You have costs, too. These costs are financial and more. The best example I can give is of my own foolishness. About 25 years ago I was remodeling a home. It had a big, old refrigerator in it that needed to be removed. However, being young and strong at the time (headstrong, that is), I decided to remove it myself.

I succeeded, at the cost of a hernia, which put me out of action for a month. It might have cost me $10 to have someone who did that sort of work for a living haul it out. So how much did it cost to have me do it?

Of course, the risk of physical injury is always an unknown. That's why I carry workers' compensation insurance and suggest you do likewise for anyone you employ. Even beyond the risk of injury, there is your time spent. Remember, your time is worth something.

■ HOW TO CALCULATE YOUR WAGES

How much is your work done on a remodeling project worth? The temptation is to say that it's not worth anything because it's done in your spare or extra time or to say that it's worth so much that you can't put a price tag on it. Both claims are evasions. Your work is worth something and it is possible to figure out how much.

The best way to do it is to think in terms of hours spent and to calculate what you might otherwise be doing and how much time (and money) you are losing by not doing that other job. For example, let's say that you're a technical writer and that you could make $600 a week, gross. Your hourly wage is $15.

If you have to take any time at all away from work, you should bill yourself at $15 an hour. If you work at remodeling in the evening and this causes you to be tired and sluggish at your regular job, resulting in errors or lost time or clients, you should bill that evening work at $15 an hour. It's taking time away from your regular job in the worst possible way.

Let's say, however, that you only remodel on the weekends or in the evening or during your vacation. In other words, you don't really take any time away from your regular job to do it. Does that mean that your time is free? I don't think so. There is still a cost there. If you weren't remodeling, could you be taking in other work on the side and making extra money?

My own feeling is that although it's difficult to pinpoint the exact value of your time spent away from your regular job, it is valuable. To my way of thinking, the only realistic way to bill it is at your regular hourly rate. If you are a technical writer, even if you aren't taking time away from your work, you are still worth at least $15 an hour.

Thus, we arrive at a working wage for you as a remodeler. Your remodeling work is worth what you otherwise earn, on an hourly basis, at your regular work.

■ AN UNFAIR METHOD?

I'm sure some readers are thinking that my method of calculating work-worth is unfair and arbitrary, particularly when it comes to extra time. Those of you who feel that way may be right. I would argue that if I'm erring, it's probably on the side of not claiming enough!

How much is time spent away from the family worth? How much are you willing to sell your extra time for? Shouldn't it be sold for more than regular time spent at work? After all, aren't you worth more when you work for yourself than when you work for someone else?

My point is that most people terribly underrate the value of their work. Chances are your time spent remodeling is worth far more than you think. If you weren't remodeling, might you not be out there doing something else that could earn you even more money?

Of course, a lot depends on how industrious you are. But it would be a mistake to discount the value of your work. Your time is a valuable commodity. The very fact that you're reading this book on remodeling proves your industriousness.

HOW TO CALCULATE YOUR HOURLY WAGE FOR REHABBING

Calculate your hourly wage at work and use that figure.

■ COMPARING YOUR COST WITH A PROFESSIONAL'S

Remembering that a pro will probably not cost you as much as you think and that your labor is probably more valuable than you may at first believe, we're now ready to make some judgment calls.

1. Determine how long it will take to do the job.

There are many ways of doing this; however, I suggest the following. First, find out how long a pro will take. This means calling someone out to give you an estimate.

Next, determine how long you will take. If you're not a pro, my suggestion is that you double the pro's time, maybe more if you're dealing with a job that's unfamiliar to you.

Pro's hours _____

Your hours _____

2. Next, multiply your hours by your hourly wage, as determined earlier. For example, if it's going to take you ten hours and your hourly wage is $15, it's a $150 job if you do it.

Your hours _____

(Your hourly wage) x _____

Job cost $ _____

3. Now compare that with how much the pro will charge. If the pro's charge is even close to what it will cost you, it's no call. Have him or her do it.

On the other hand, if the pro wants $500 to do the work and you figure you can do it for $100, then it's a different story. (Even so, don't forget to factor in the risk of injury as well as the risk of the job not coming out as well if you do it.)

Your cost $ _____

Pro's cost $ _____

I'm sure that if you're like me, even after this elaborate explanation, you're going to feel it's money down the drain hiring someone else to do the work. Don't.

Remember that while the pro is doing one job, you can be doing another. The effect of having two of you working will be to shorten the time it takes to finish the remodeling.

Here's a good guideline I picked up years ago and have assiduously followed:

You don't make money by turning off the lights to save electricity. You make it by working more efficiently and increasing your income.

■ SKILLED JOBS

Finally, there's the matter of work quality. Which jobs can you really do as well as a pro and which require professionally skilled labor? You think you can do everything as well as a professional? You may be surprised by what you read in the remainder of this and following chapters.

There are certain jobs that you can learn quickly and do well enough to get by on the first or second attempt. A surprising one (to some people) is plumbing.

If you're mechanically inclined, you can learn from a book how to do almost any plumbing job required in a house. We'll learn several later on in this book. Furthermore, in most cases you know immediately whether you did it right—either it leaks or it doesn't!

On the other hand, some jobs require a lot of skill and training, such as taping plasterboard. It's as simple as putting mud (wallboard paste) and tape across a joint. Any child of ten can do it. However, doing it right so that the wall is smooth and the seam doesn't show takes practice and skill. I've done it maybe 50 times and I'm just getting to the point where I feel my work is coming close to looking professional.

If you aren't skilled at taping and texturing, it's well worth the money to get a pro to do it. It's not just the money. It's a matter of getting a finished job that looks good.

Remember, your ultimate goal isn't to save money—it's to make money and enjoy a nicer home if you choose to live there. You will make your money when you resell the house. However, it's going to be far harder to resell if the quality of work looks bad. Nothing looks worse than a wall that has been badly plastered!

Which are the jobs you should hire out because of the skill level required and which should you be able to do yourself?

There are no national surveys to tell you the answer. In fact, a lot depends on your own mechanical abilities and how quickly you can learn. What follows is my own table (Figure 5.1), compiled over the years, which may be useful as a guidepost. I'm certain you'll disagree with some of my choices, and equally certain that you'll agree with others. Just remember, it's a guide intended to give you direction, not to cast your feet in concrete.

■ PERMITS

One last question remains: Can you, as an individual, do work that normally requires a city permit? We're talking about things as simple as hooking up a dishwasher (yes, it does require a permit in most jurisdictions!) or as complex as adding on a room. Can you do it with building department permission, if you don't have a contractor's license or have not passed tests of skill in the area?

The answer is yes—and no. The answer is no, usually, if you are doing it as a business not on your own property. It's usually yes if you are the owner-occupant of the property.

I have never heard of any jurisdiction that refused a permit to an owner-occupant of a building to do any kind of construction work from the simplest to the most complex. As long as you can demonstrate that you are living in the property and own it, you should be able to get a permit.

Just on the outside chance that your jurisdiction is an exception, check with the appropriate county or city building department to be sure. Also, keep in mind that some jurisdictions require special assurances from you. For example, they may require that you do all the work yourself. If you hire any of it out, they may require you to obtain workers' compensation to protect the workers in case of accident. They may also require you to sign a statement that you intend to live on the property for at least six months.

FIGURE 5.1 ■ Guide to Skill Levels

JOB	DEGREE OF DIFFICULTY FOR A BEGINNER (1 IS EASIEST; 10 IS HARDEST)
Air conditioner, fix	6
Air conditioner, install	3
Bath, faucets, install	1
Bath, lights, install	3
Bath, plumbing, fix	2
Bath, sink, fix	2
Bath, sink, install	3
Bath, tile, install	8
Bath, toilet, install	3
Bath, tub/shower, fix	2
Bath, tub/shower glass doors, install	2
Bath, tub/shower, install	6
Carpet, install	3
Carpet, padding, install	1
Carpet, shampoo	1
Carport, build	5
Carport, design	2
Ceiling beams, fix	6
Ceiling beams, replace	9
Chisel	4
Countertop, install	8
Deck, cement	8
Deck, layout	2
Deck, wood, build frame	2

FIGURE 5.1   *(continued)*

Deck, wood, nail flooring	T
Deck, wood, sink post holes	T
Door handles, replace	T
Door, sliding glass, handle, replace	T
Door, sliding glass, replace	TTT
Doorbell, fix	T
Doorbell, install	TT
Dormer, cut and support roof	TTTTTTT
Dormer, design	TTTTTT
Dormer, install	TTTTTTTTT
Drill, electric	TT
Fence, wood, fix	T
Fence, wood, install	TTT
Fireplace, brick, build	TTTTTTTTT
Fireplace, clean	TT
Fireplace, ready-made, install	TTTTTTT
Fireplace, replace chipped mortar	TTT
Floor, linoleum, install	TTTTT
Floor, preparation	T
Floor, strengthen, straighten	TTTTTTT
Floor, tile, ceramic	TTTT
Floor, tile, self-adhesive	TTT
Floor, wood, hardwood, even piece, nail	TTTTTTTT
Floor, wood, random plank, glue	TTT
Floor, wood, random plank, nail	TTTTTTTT

FIGURE 5.1 *(continued)*

Furnace, central, installation	⊤⊤⊤⊤⊤⊤⊤
Garbage disposal, install	⊤⊤⊤⊤
Gutters, install	⊤⊤⊤
Hammer	⊤⊤⊤
Heater, peripheral, installation	⊤⊤⊤⊤
House, lift, level	⊤⊤⊤⊤⊤⊤⊤⊤⊤⊤
Insulation	⊤⊤
Kitchen, cabinet, new, install	⊤⊤
Kitchen, cabinet, paint	⊤⊤
Kitchen, cabinet, refinish	⊤⊤⊤
Kitchen, cabinet, resurface	⊤⊤⊤⊤⊤⊤⊤⊤⊤
Kitchen, dishwasher, install	⊤⊤
Kitchen, garbage disposal, install	⊤⊤⊤
Kitchen, light fixtures, recessed	⊤⊤⊤⊤⊤
Kitchen, light fixtures, surface	⊤
Kitchen, linoleum, sheet	⊤⊤⊤⊤⊤⊤⊤⊤⊤
Kitchen, linoleum, squares	⊤⊤
Kitchen, sink drain, fix/install	⊤⊤⊤
Kitchen, stove/oven, install	⊤⊤⊤
Light fixture, install	⊤
Paint	⊤
Patio, brick, mortar	⊤⊤⊤⊤
Patio, brick, no mortar	⊤
Patio, concrete, finish	⊤⊤⊤⊤⊤⊤⊤
Patio, concrete, pour	⊤⊤

FIGURE 5.1 *(continued)*

Patio, frame for concrete	T
Patio, install wire or steel	T
Plaster	TTTTTTTT
Plumbing ABC, glue, sewer	T
Plumbing, copper, solder	TT
Plumbing, galvanized steel, thread, fit	TTTTTT
Plumbing PVC, glue	T
Plumbing sewer line, dig up, fix	TTTTT
Porch/deck, build	TTT
Porch/deck, design	TT
Porch, screen, enclose	TT
Roof, tar & gravel, redo	TT
Roof, tar-shingles, fix	TT
Roof, tile, fix	TTTT
Roof, tile, replace	TTTTTTT
Roof, wood, shingles, fix	TT
Roof, wood, shingles, replace	TTTTT
Room, add	TTTTTTTTT
Sanding, electric belt	TTTT
Sanding, electric, rotary	TT
Sanding, electric, rotary—floor	TTT
Sanding, hand	T
Sawing, electric	TTT
Sheet rock, finish	TTTTTT
Sheet rock, install	TT

FIGURE 5.1 *(continued)*

Sheet rock, nail	T
Sheet rock, tape	TTTT
Skylight, fix	TT
Skylight, install	TTTTT
Slab, cracks, level floor	TTTTT
Slab, cracks, patch	T
Spa, install	TTT
Spa, plumbing, fix	TTT
Sprinklers, fix	T
Sprinklers, install	TT
Sprinklers, install automatic system	TT
Stairs, carpeting, fix	TT
Stairs, fix individual	T
Stairs, supports, fix	TTTTT
Stove/oven, electric, install	TTT
Stove/oven, gas, install	TTTT
Toilet, fix	TT
Toilet, install	T
Wall, block, fix	TT
Wall, block, install	TTTTT
Wall, brick, fix	TT
Wall, brick, install	TTTTT
Wall, interior, move	TTTTTTTT
Wall, interior, remove	TTTTTTTT
Wall, plaster	TTTTTTT

FIGURE 5.1   *(continued)*

Wall, siding—exterior, install	𝖳 𝖳 𝖳
Wall, stucco	𝖳 𝖳 𝖳 𝖳 𝖳 𝖳 𝖳
Wall, wood—exterior, install	𝖳 𝖳 𝖳
Wallpaper	𝖳 𝖳 𝖳
Water heater, install	𝖳 𝖳 𝖳
Window, box, install (enlarge wall)	𝖳 𝖳 𝖳 𝖳 𝖳 𝖳 𝖳 𝖳 𝖳
Window, new, install	𝖳 𝖳 𝖳 𝖳 𝖳 𝖳 𝖳
Window, replace	𝖳 𝖳 𝖳
Window, screens, install	𝖳
Window, screens, replace screen	𝖳
Window, storm, install	𝖳 𝖳 𝖳

■ ═ C H A P T E R 6 ═ ■

Remodeling Bathrooms

The bathroom is probably the next most important feature of a home to most people after the kitchen and entrance. In some ways it is the most important because the quality and style of the bathroom define the quality (and often the value) of the house. When it comes time to resell, a remodeled bathroom is often worth its price in a quick sale. Therefore, time spent remodeling a bathroom is usually not wasted.

In this chapter we are going to look at a number of specific bathroom problems and how to solve them. Please keep in mind that bathroom problems run the gamut from the simplest to the most complex.

Most of the work suggested is to be done on the central or main bathroom, the one people use most when they come into the house. You may want to do some work on the master and guest bathrooms as well. In my experience, if your main bathroom is outstanding, lesser quality in other bathrooms is usually forgiven.

Keep in mind that my purpose here is not to give a detailed explanation of how to do the work. There are many illustrated books on the market that do a good job of that. Here, we're trying to determine what's involved, how hard it is, how much it will cost, whether an average person can do it and what to watch out for. We are looking for a way to decide whether to make the improvement.

■ INSTALLING A SLIDING GLASS DOOR IN A TUB/SHOWER

■ *PROBLEM*

Tub/shower enclosure is old, but not dilapidated. Existing tile is not broken but the entire tub, with shower over it, does not look appealing or modern.

■ *SOLUTION*

Many old homes rely on a rod and shower curtain over the tub/shower. It costs very little to replace the curtain, but a new shower curtain isn't going to modernize the home. One of the easiest ways to spruce up a tub/shower is to add a sliding glass stall door. A new stall door immediately modernizes the tub/shower area and makes even older tile sparkle.

Cost

Stall doors are readily available at any building supply and vary enormously in price. The least expensive is likely to be around $50 with the price going up to as much as $1,000 for gold-trimmed, ornate models.

The model you get should be appropriate to the house you are remodeling. For example, if you are working on a moderately priced home that has chrome bathroom trim in the towel racks and toilet handle and linoleum tile on the floor, you will probably want a modestly priced chrome stall door. Nice models are selling in the neighborhood of $100.

On the other hand, if you're dealing with an upscale home that has gold trim and oak (or other wood) in the bathroom, you will want to get a gold-trimmed tub/shower door as well. Of course, you will have to pay considerably more.

Models are also available in anodized bronze, antique and a variety of finishes. If your tile inside isn't wonderful, I suggest avoiding clear glass and instead opting for opaque glass, possibly with a pattern. Always insist on safety plate glass.

Installation and Degree of Difficulty

Installation is easy and can be done in an hour or two even by an inexperienced worker. All that's required is to drill three or more holes into brackets on the side walls. The brackets are then screwed into place, with the bottom being held securely by caulk and the top usually held in place by gravity. The doors are then easily installed.

What To Watch Out for When Installing

Be careful when you drill the holes for the brackets. If you have to drill through tile, use a special ceramic drill bit or the tile may crack. If possible, try to drill in the grooves, or grout (caulk) areas, between tiles.

Be sure that the grout placed under the bottom sill forms a good seal to prevent water from leaking out. Be sure the bottom sill is correctly placed—the little holes face inward so water collecting in the grooves runs back into the tub. Finish off with a thin bead of caulk along the inside and outside edges of the sill. To smooth the caulk, wet your finger with water and then press it along the bead. The caulk will smooth out for a professional look.

Use a helper to lift the glass doors; they can be quite heavy. Usually they require some adjustment at the top to make them level.

Typical cost of materials	$200
Time to complete	2 hours
Degree of difficulty	*T T*
Do-it-yourself/Hire someone	**DO IT** ~~HIRE OUT~~

■ INSTALLING A SINK/VANITY

■ *PROBLEM*

Existing sink may be cracked, discolored or cheap-looking. You want to improve the appearance of the bathroom, and the sink is often the first place people look.

■ *SOLUTION*

Install a new sink and possibly a new vanity. There are really only two ways to go here, either a minimal installation or a deluxe. I always suggest the deluxe installation.

In a minimal installation, you will probably buy a white, porcelain-on-steel 18-inch sink. The sink is typically supported from the wall by a bracket and the plumbing hangs down underneath. The shorter the plumbing lines, the less visible they are. The faucets will be the cheapest chrome available. In a deluxe installation, you buy a vanity that holds the sink. The sink may be a molded top made of cultured (synthetic) marble or it may be a marble top with a cutaway in which you can place a carved or specially colored porcelain sink. The faucets may be gold with wood or porcelain trim.

Cost

Standard wall-hanging porcelain sinks are available for around $50 or less. Minimal chrome plumbing (today, usually chromed plastic) can be obtained for around $25.

For a much more modern and appealing presentation, use a vanity. These are readily available in a variety of woods at most large discount hardware stores. A typical oak vanity with cultured marble top can be obtained for under $250 as of this writing. Cut the price by up to 50 percent if you buy on sale. On the other hand, if you have the cabinet built to order, expect to pay up to three times as much. Fancy gold or wood-trimmed porcelain plumbing fixtures are quite expensive. Expect to pay a minimum of $50; for deluxe fixtures, the cost can easily go to several hundred dollars. I recommend the lower end.

Installation and Degree of Difficulty

The installation of the wall-hanging sink is tricky, but not difficult. It requires bolting a metal bracket into studs and then hanging the sink from it.

The installation of the vanity is simple. You just get it into the bathroom and nail through the back supports into the studs. The marble top usually just fits on top and is held in place by gravity, caulk and the plumbing.

The plumbing is tricky. Assuming that you are not going into the wall to change the location of the plumbing outlets, you must do the following:

1. Install the faucets to the sink or marbleized top.

2. Connect tubing to the hot and cold shutoff valves (assuming they are already in place).

3. Connect the drain to the existing drain opening.

The work requires a moderate amount of plumbing skill. There will probably be no pipe threading or soldering involved. All the joints will be compression with rubber or plastic washers.

What To Watch Out for When Installing

With the wall-hanging sink, the only problem you are likely to have will occur if you don't mount the holding bracket directly into studs behind the wall. It must be mounted into studs. Using molly bolts (which are self-adhering, used on plasterboard) or other wallboard holders will not work, especially when a child climbs up onto the sink, putting enormous pressure on the bracket. It's better to move the sink to line up with two studs than to take a chance hanging the sink on just one.

The only problem with the vanity installation is likely to occur in measurement. Be sure the vanity is small enough to fit the space available in the bathroom. Also, be sure that it will get through the bathroom door. You probably will have to cut a small portion out of the bottom side walls of the vanity to accommodate the baseboard.

The plumbing can be difficult if it's your first time. The easiest way to do it is to connect the faucets to the sink before you install the sink. Otherwise, you'll be crawling around underneath trying to get the fittings on.

For the tubes connecting to the hot/cold shutoff valves, use nylon flexible hoses. They are much easier to work with than the older style metal, which had to be bent carefully and correctly. Be sure to get hoses that aren't too long.

For the drain, use plastic pipe where possible. It's much easier to handle. Today, traps and other drain materials are all available in plastic.

Once the sink is installed, you won't be able to tighten the fittings on the hoses or the faucets using standard wrenches because there won't be room. However, there is a special plumber's helper wrench that is offset and that fits underneath the sink to do the job. Ask at your local hardware store. They usually cost less than $5.

Typical cost of materials	$100–$400
Time to complete	12 hours
Degree of difficulty	*T T T*
Do-it-yourself/Hire someone	**DO IT** OR **HIRE OUT**

■ INSTALLING NEW FAUCET HANDLES

■ *PROBLEM*

The faucet handles on the sink, tub and shower are old-fashioned, they are caked with paint from earlier botched remodeling work by previous owners, or they are rusted, caked with mineral deposits or otherwise broken or ugly.

■ *SOLUTION*

Replace the faucet handles. New handles and spigots are available for the most common brands such as Delta or Price Pfister. A good hardware store can sell you replacement parts. Just by putting on new faucet handles, you can spruce up the appearance of a sink, shower and tub.

Cost

Replacement faucet handles and matching spigots aren't cheap. However, they are well worth the cost for the improvement they make. Many discount hardware stores don't specialize enough to carry exact replacement parts. Instead, they offer "universal" faucet replacements. These usually don't fit on precisely, but instead must be held in place with a little retaining screw. Their cost is usually minimal, perhaps $5 a pair. My advice is to stay away from these. Although they may appear to do the job, they will quickly fail with use, and the problem will come back to haunt you.

Installation and Degree of Difficulty

Remove the old faucets, usually by lifting a cap on the top and taking out a single screw. Then lift them off and replace with new ones. The degree of difficulty is minimal.

What To Watch Out for When Installing

The biggest problem is getting the old faucets off. Often rust or mineral deposits have built up, making it almost impossible to remove them.

Because you are going to discard them anyway, you may end up using a claw hammer to get them off. Just be careful not to damage whatever you're using as a wedge against the back of the hammer.

Another method I have found useful when faucets are hard to remove is to try to get a pair of pliers behind or under them to loosen the seat, and then remove the seat with the faucet attached. You can take the assembly to a workshop where you can use a vice or other tools to pry the old faucet off.

Typical cost of materials	$10-$50
Time to complete	1/2 hour
Degree of difficulty	T
Do-it-yourself/Hire someone	**DO IT** ~~HIRE OUT~~

■ INSTALLING A TOILET

■ *PROBLEM*

The existing toilet is old-fashioned, cracked or stained. It is either unserviceable or unsightly.

■ *SOLUTION*

Replace the entire toilet. There are really no alternatives here. It is simply better to get rid of a problem toilet than to try any kind of repair. (Note: We are talking about the toilet itself, not just the plumbing inside.)

Cost

Even today you can pick up an inexpensive toilet complete with all the internal plumbing installed and ready to operate for less than $75. Of course, for that price you don't get a deluxe unit. Often the toilet is smaller than you would like and the flushing action may require more water than many of the new water-savers. However, this minimal toilet, usually available only in white, is quite serviceable and most buyers can't really tell the difference between it and a more expensive toilet.

A deluxe toilet can be quite expensive. I've seen models that cost nearly $2,000! Typically these have unusual shapes, colors and moldings, and their flushing action (I presume) is excellent. If yours is a deluxe remodel, you will definitely want to consider a deluxe toilet. Note: With a deluxe toilet the inner workings and handle are frequently not included, but must be purchased and installed separately. A gold-plated handle alone can cost $50 or more.

Installation and Degree of Difficulty

Although most people suppose that a toilet is difficult to install, it is actually the easiest of all the bathroom appliances. It is held by only two bolts, which attach to the upper flange of the sewer pipe, level with the floor. Simply remove the old toilet, put the new one in place, being sure to get the wax seal properly seated and to get the two screws (obtained for a dollar or so) coming through the holes, and then tighten. If the tank comes separate, place it on the toilet bowl supports, insert the thick rubber washer in the drain hole, and then tighten the two screws that hold the tank on. For the water supply, use a nylon flex-hose of the correct length. The entire hookup, barring problems, should take less than an hour.

What To Watch Out for When Installing

It can take several hours if you have problems. The first problem is likely to be removing the old toilet. Often the two screws holding it to the sewer flange are rusted and will not unscrew. Because you are going to discard the old toilet, my suggestion is to either cut off the screws using a hacksaw or break the toilet porcelain around the screws, making them easier to get out. If you break the porcelain, watch out for razor-sharp edges that could cut you.

One big problem is when the flange from the sewer line is damaged. This flange bolts onto the floor. If it's damaged (so that you can't get new toilet bolts onto it), you'll have to remove it. With black plastic pipe, simply cut through the line below the flange. Then glue on a union, a new piece of pipe and a new flange, which you will attach to the floor. With older metal pipe, it's much more difficult and you may want a plumber's help. You'll have to convert to plastic, using a pressure clamp fitting over the old pipe. Or you'll have to install a new flange using old cast-iron pipe, tamping in hemp and then filling with liquid lead. This latter operation is a tricky job not done much anymore because of the danger of lead poisoning from the fumes.

When you tighten the tank to the toilet bowl and the toilet itself to the floor, be sure you don't overtighten, or you could crack the porcelain. Be sure the toilet bottom is flush with the floor. If it is uneven, tightening the toilet even slightly could cause it to crack. Also, if it is uneven, the toilet will wobble when someone sits on it. When tightening the tank to the toilet bowl, be sure to use the rubber grommets that come with the bolts. They go inside the tank and ensure that water doesn't leak out around the fitting.

Typical cost of materials	$75-$1,000
Time to complete	1–2 hours
Degree of difficulty	𝘛 𝘛 𝘛
Do-it-yourself/Hire someone	**DO IT** ~~HIRE OUT~~

■ INSTALLING A NEW TUB/SHOWER

■ *PROBLEM*

The existing tub, shower or combo is unappealing. The tile could be cracked, the tub or shower could be stained, usually with rust, and the fixtures could be old-fashioned.

■ *SOLUTION*

Renovate the existing tub. If the tub is the only problem, you can hire someone to resurface the porcelain. This works well and the results are amazing. Tub refinishers are listed in the yellow pages of the phone book. However, it should be done only if there are no major problems with the tile or the drain. If you have to replace the tile around the tub, you're better off replacing the tub as well (and it's a lot cheaper).

Installing a new tub/shower involves removing the old tub/shower, the old tile or other wall coverings and the old fixtures and perhaps going into the wall to install new valves and drains. The job is complex, especially if you attempt to move the location of the tub/shower. I suggest that, if at all possible, you retain the old position.

Cost

Having a tub refinished costs about $250 as of this writing. It takes about a day and another three or four days to dry and age properly.

Installing a new tub/shower is a major bathroom renovation and therefore can be costly. It doesn't have to be, however. To put in a new tub/shower, new fixtures and new wall coverings, you can hire out and have a deluxe job done, easily costing $3,000 or more. If you do it yourself, however, the price can be surprisingly small.

I recently did a tub/shower combination installation. I bought a new white porcelain tub on sale at a hardware discount house for $75. The walls consisted of a three-piece fiberglass product that glued onto the existing "green board" (a special type of wallboard that is mold- and mildew-resistant) and cost about $135. New faucets and other fixtures cost about $50. The entire installation (parts only) came to less than $400 and it looked terrific!

Installation and Degree of Difficulty

In some ways the hardest part is removing the existing tub/shower, which, along with the old tile or other covering, will have to be taken out. I suggest taking everything out right down to the studs. Getting into the wall allows you to see the water valves and determine whether the washers can be replaced or whether an entirely new valve faucet is needed. If a new one is needed, you may need to solder it in.

Once the old material is out, the new tub should be installed, then the fixtures (such as the rough valves) and finally the green board. Next, you'll need to install the wall covering (typically fiberglass or tile), and the job will be finished.

Installing a tub/shower requires a lot of confidence, but not a great deal of skill. With the exception of installing tile, no high level of skill is required. However, the work is heavy and messy, and when things don't fit, it can be quite frustrating.

What To Watch Out for When Installing

If you need to install a new faucet and valves, keep in mind that because you're putting in a new wall, they do not need to be in exactly the same vertical position as the old. If your new tub is wider or narrower than the old, you will want to reposition the faucets so they are centered.

One of the most difficult parts of the job is getting the old tub out. Tubs are typically porcelain over metal and may weigh several hundred pounds. On top of that, the typical bathroom is five feet wide, and the tub is also that width, so you can't really angle it out without hitting the walls. One solution is to use a sledgehammer to dent in the sides of the old tub. This will allow it to slip out more freely. Be sure to wear safety glasses when working with the sledgehammer.

Don't try to get a single-piece fiberglass tub/shower, even though they are readily available at reduced prices. These must be installed at the time the house is built and will not fit into a finished bathroom through the door. If you insist on using a single-piece unit, you may have to remove the outer wall of the bathroom to get it in!

Be careful with the drain under the tub when removing the old unit. Typically an old installation will be rusted and the drain may break when you try to separate it from the old tub. If it looks as if it may break, you may want to cut it a short distance below the tub. A clean cut will be easier to fix with a compression fitting than a long, jagged tear, which might result if you try to flex it out.

Be sure that the faucet handles are the right size so that they fit close to the wall but do not touch it.

If you use a fiberglass wall covering, I suggest that you get one that is in at least three pieces. This allows for flexibility when installing. If you use tile, see the next section on tile installation.

Typical cost of materials	$400-1,500
Time to complete	30 hours
Degree of difficulty	*T T T T T*
Do-it-yourself/Hire someone	**DO IT** OR **HIRE OUT**

■ INSTALLING NEW FLOOR/WALL TILE

■ PROBLEM

Tiles are often a must for any kind of high-quality remodel. The existing tile may be cracked, discolored or the wrong color, or the current wall or floor coverings may not be tile. In some cases a previous owner has self-installed tile, and although the condition of the tile is okay, the installation itself looks amateurish.

■ SOLUTION

First, check to see whether you can save the existing tile. Sometimes the problem is limited to one small area. You may be able to replace the tile in that area and save the rest. (Note: Don't waste time trying to match old tile—you can't.) There are only two solutions to a small area of tile that's bad: Take existing tile from some area that's not noticeable, or replace a logical small area of tile with new. For example, in a shower stall the floor tile may be bad, but the walls may be okay. Instead of replacing all the tile, replace only the floor tiles with a complementary color. (Sometimes you can do this as an accent around the edge of the tile even if it isn't damaged!)

Do install new tile. Nothing looks more deluxe than tile. For walls and floors in both bath and kitchen, it is an excellent high-quality installation.

New tiles, particularly colored tiles (including the new Japanese tiles with striking colors) in blue, green and beige, lend a truly high-quality appeal to the property. Beware of using the wrong size of tile. Many stores sell tiny one-inch tiles attached to one-foot-square woven matrices of nylon. They are sold on the basis that it's a lot easier to install an entire foot of tile than a single one-inch-square piece. The trouble is that everyone has seen these tiny tiles, and generally speaking they mean an amateur installation. I would stay away from them. Quality wall and counter installations use $3' \times 3'$, $4' \times 4'$, or $6' \times 6'$ tiles. Floor installations can use the larger one-foot-square tiles. Of course, the larger the tiles, the fewer you'll have to install!

There are many types of tile to choose from, including glazed, unglazed and quarry. Go to a large tile store and look at their selection to get an idea of the different types available. I always use a shiny, glazed finish for bathrooms—most people expect to see that kind of tile there. (Note: See the section on tile countertop installation in Chapter 7.)

Cost

Tile is expensive, regardless of who does the work. A high-quality, professional installation in a bathroom or kitchen can easily cost from $1,500 to $5,000 or more, including labor and materials.

Because tile work is labor-intensive, you can save a great deal by doing it yourself. The cost of materials varies enormously depending on the quality of tile that you get. Italian tiles are probably the most treasured, but the Japanese and other oriental tiles are probably the best for the money these days.

Installation and Degree of Difficulty

Keep in mind that a fairly high level of skill is involved in installing tile. I've done dozens of tile installations, and I'm just now getting so that the job looks professional. Nevertheless, if you're careful and don't use small tiles, a fairly acceptable job can be done the first time. Beware of walls, however; they are much harder to do than floors. (For countertops, see Chapter 7.)

Remove all the existing wall or floor coverings down to either base floor or the wall studs. Chances are there will be black mold if there was any moisture leakage at all. This should be scraped off and sprayed with a mildew inhibitor. A moisture barrier may be needed if moisture is coming through the wall (for example, an outside wall below ground level).

Prepare walls by installing green board or, in nonwet installations, "wonder board" (gypsum wallboard with holes that allow mortar to hold). Tile may also be affixed directly to cement or to a mortar bed (see Chapter 7 on counters). Make sure all surfaces are perfectly flat and level. Prepare floors by thoroughly cleaning them and using special chemical sealers.

Stores that sell tile will also sell you adhesive and rent you all the equipment you need for installation, including cutters. Be sure to use only the special adhesive that is recommended for tiles (usually thin-set, mastic or epoxy, depending on your application) and to follow directions carefully.

"Bunt-nose" tile can be used for corners, but each piece must be specially bought, and it is difficult, if not impossible, to cut. A guideline should be drawn for your first row, but give special care to how edges will come out: You don't want uneven or cut rows in front. Special plastic corner guides can be used to give the tiles equal spacing.

After you have installed the tiles, grout using a special rubber-backed trowel. Then remove excess grout and clean.

What To Watch Out for When Installing

The level of skill required is high; consequently, there are dozens of things to watch out for when installing tile. Here are just a few.

Make sure the walls and floors are cleaned and sealed, or the tile may loosen later on. Pay special attention to leveling, as any bumps or imperfections will make the tiles uneven.

Plan to go slowly. Even professional tile workers can take days to install a bathroom. Just remember that this is a process in which you put in one tile after another. As long as you're careful that each piece fits where it's supposed to, you should come out okay. Trying to hurry makes for a terrible job.

Typically the store that sells you the tile will lend or rent you a snap tile cutter. (You will need to cut some tile in order to make things fit.) These operate by scratching the title and then breaking it along the scratch. In some ways, these tile cutters require as much skill to use as does correctly placing the tile on floors or walls. You may ruin so much tile using these that you will want to throw up your hands in despair. (I've often suspected that the tile stores lend these so freely because they know the buyer will have to come back for more tile to make up for the broken pieces!)

Although professional installers can use these cutters effectively, if it's your first time it may well be worth the cost to rent an electric tile cutter. (Most equipment stores rent them.) These have diamond blades and allow you to quickly and accurately make almost any cut. Most pros use this electric equipment.

The corner spacers will determine how wide the groove is between tiles. Don't try for a very narrow groove (1/4 inch or less). You might think it looks good, but getting the tile down accurately and then getting the grout in the grooves can be a real headache.

Finally, once you've pressed the grout into place (use cement-based grout for most applications—you can use silicone rubber caulk, but the tile will not be rigid and can move slightly), be sure you remove enough from the tops of the grooves. The biggest mistake first-timers make is not removing enough grout from the tops of the grooves. It's easy to do when the grout is fresh and soft, but impossible once it dries.

You want to give the grout between the tiles a nice concave shape and not to bulge out. The way to do this is to remove the grout from the groove to just below the surface of the tile. Usually, the first time you try this you'll think you're removing too much grout. Chances are you're not.

For additional information, I recommend the Sunset book *Tile*. There are many books out on the subject, but this one seems to give the clearest explanations.

Typical cost of materials	$1–$12 per sq. ft.
Time to complete	35 hours
Degree of difficulty	*7 7 7 7 7 7 7*
Do-it-yourself/Hire someone	**DO IT** ~~HIRE OUT~~

■ FIXING LEAKY PLUMBING

■ *PROBLEM*

Pipes leak under the sink, behind the tub or shower or in the walls or floor. The toilet runs after it's flushed or effluent comes out from under the toilet after flushing.

■ *SOLUTION*

Fix the leaking systems. Instead of reinstalling new fixtures, tubs and showers, as described above, here we're concerned with simply fixing existing problems.

Cost

If you do it yourself, the cost of materials is usually negligible. If you call in a plumber, you can expect to pay the hourly wage for your area. In some parts of the country, a range of $65 to $100 an hour is typical.

I don't like doing these jobs if the leaks are in the wall and involve galvanized pipe. I usually hire this kind of work out, first getting a total-cost bid.

Installation and Degree of Difficulty

Usually water leaks are caused by washer seals that fail or are defective. Replace the washer or seal and the leak will vanish. This task requires little skill, but it can sometimes be surprisingly difficult and can take an amazing amount of time.

If the leak is in the wall or floor, it may be caused by a rusted joint or a burst pipe (usually a delayed effect from a winter freeze). In this case a section of wall may have to be removed. You may have to go into the basement or crawl space or remove a section of ceiling under the floor where the problem is. For galvanized pipe it usually means unscrewing the pipe (using large pipe wrenches) and, working back from the outlet to the leak, replacing with new pipe. Copper pipe is much easier to work with. The troublesome section can simply be removed and a new section soldered in.

In the case of a plastic drain, a section can be cut out and a new section glued in. For a metal drain, I find it easier to cut out the old section and use compression fittings on both ends and then replace the damaged portion with plastic.

For toilets, a wax seal is used under the bowl. Remove the screws that hold the bowl to the floor and lift. Scrape out the old seal using a putty knife and then press a new seal into place. Refit the bowl to the floor.

What To Watch Out for When Installing

Sometimes a leak in galvanized pipe can be sealed using a metal-and-rubber compression fitting, sold at most hardware stores. This fits over the break and then screws into place. It provides only a temporary solution because the fitting will rust out eventually.

When screwing fittings on, try using Teflon tape or paste. It makes an excellent sealer and allows the fitting to be easily screwed on.

If at all possible, try to fix a leak in a shower or tub faucet rather than replacing the valve. To replace it, you may have to take out a portion of a wall, requiring a great deal of work. Try grinding the seat, putting in a new washer or buying a new insert, any of which may work.

When installing a toilet wax seal, there's a good chance you'll get some effluent on your hands, and this could result in a rash or even a more severe infection. One trick is to use plastic surgical gloves—you can still manipulate parts easily, but your hands are protected.

Be aware that when working with old galvanized pipe, you are taking a big risk in creating new leaks. Old steel pipe inevitably rusts inside. Every time you put a plumber's wrench onto it you risk distorting and cracking the metal, causing a new leak. For this reason, I prefer to use compression fittings where possible, and when not, to rely on the services of a professional plumber. The headaches avoided are well worth any additional cost!

Typical cost of materials	$1-$50
Time to complete	1-10 hours
Degree of difficulty	$T\,T$
Do-it-yourself/Hire someone	**DO IT** ~~HIRE OUT~~

■ INSTALLING NEW LIGHTS

■ *PROBLEM*

Many bathrooms are drab and dreary places. Often the only natural light comes from a tiny window. Sometimes there isn't even a window.

When many older houses were built, the bathroom was given a single overhead light, often with only one incandescent bulb. Costly improvements such as new tile or a new tub/shower may go unnoticed by prospective buyers without good lighting to highlight the features.

■ *SOLUTION*

Probably the most overlooked solution to improving a bathroom is the lighting. Lighting sets the mood for the bathroom, and lots of light gives the room an upbeat, warm, high-quality look. Often, a small, unimpressive bathroom can be made to feel larger and more luxurious simply by adding corrective lighting.

Most building codes today require fluorescent lighting in bathrooms, both because of the even, bright quality and because of their economical use. However, I find that although fluorescents give a lot of light, that light tends to be very harsh and not warm. It is a cold light that can make the bathroom look cold.

I always add a lot of incandescent lights to a bathroom. Particularly nice are the makeup lights that are now widely sold at hardware stores. These are placed around mirrors and have large bulbs that do not require a fixture. Women often appreciate having the extra light around the mirrors to help with makeup.

I also add a bigger light fixture in the ceiling. Typically a fixture that holds 150 watts will do. The whole idea is to be able to turn on the bathroom switch and have the room explode with light. If the walls are freshly painted and all fixtures new or at least spotlessly clean, the light will show them off. It's a selling feature that is one of the quickest and easiest to install.

Cost

If you already have the electrical outlets, sockets and switches in place, the cost is simply that of the fixtures. For a complete bathroom setup, the fixtures at a hardware discount shouldn't run much more than $50, or $100 for fancier ones.

If you need to install electrical connections, the cost for materials is usually low, typically less than $25. Unless you do it yourself, however, expect to pay several hundred for an electrician.

Installation and Degree of Difficulty

Installing fixtures usually means unscrewing the old one and screwing the new one in. For some fixtures, you'll have to add holding screws into the walls or ceiling. The degree of difficulty is low.

If you need to move wiring, however, you must be up on the local electrical building codes. You'll also need an electrical permit from your local building department. The installation of wiring in a bathroom is not difficult, but it is precise. All wiring must be grounded, for safety reasons, and many areas require GFI (Ground Fault

Interrupter) circuits. Also, the building department may require specific hookups.

The actual work is not difficult, although it may require that you break out some wallboard to move wires through studs and then to replace the wall. It's a good idea to have an experienced electrician or handyperson show you how the first time.

What To Watch Out for When Installing

If you need to break into walls to move wiring, try to remove wallboard only between studs. That way, you'll have something to nail the new wallboard onto.

When you have wiring coming out of boxes, leave enough so that it can be stripped, and then bend the excess wire back into the box with the socket or fixture attached. When you add the socket or fixture, cut off most of the wire so the rest will fit back into the box.

The electrical codes are quite straightforward. Get a code book at your local bookstore to give you information on how to deal with wiring. Also, someone at the local building department may be willing to spend some time explaining how to do it.

Typical cost of materials	$75-$150
Time to complete	1-2 hours
Degree of difficulty	TTT
Do-it-yourself/Hire someone	**DO IT** ~~HIRE OUT~~

Bathrooms are not usually the easiest area of the house to renovate because they are small and difficult to get into, but the results reflect well on the whole property.

■ ═══ CHAPTER 7 ═══ ■

Considering Kitchen Solutions

The place where most people gather in a house is the kitchen. The old adage is that the kitchen sells the house is true to a great extent. A great-looking kitchen can overcome a lot of detracting features elsewhere.

In this chapter we are going to look at a number of kitchen remodeling problems and solutions. Please keep in mind, however, that kitchen problems are as varied as kitchens themselves. We'll just deal with the most generic here.

Also keep in mind that our purpose here is not to give a detailed explanation of how to do the work. There are many illustrated books on the market that do a good job of that. Here, we're trying to determine just what's involved, how hard it is, how much it will cost, whether an average person can do it, and what to watch out for.

■ INSTALLING NEW COUNTERTOPS

■ *PROBLEM*

The existing countertops are unattractive. If they are tile, they are cracked, and the grout is discolored. If Formica, the surface is worn, burnt, discolored or peeling. If some other surface, it looks old-fashioned.

■ *SOLUTION*

Redo the countertop. The first question should be Can the existing countertop be saved?

If it is tile, the biggest problem is likely to be the edges. The edges take the worst abuse with things bumped against them. Most cracks show up there. If the remaining tile is intact, you may be able to avoid a big job by doing a clever small one.

Remove the edge tile (assuming you have distinct edge pieces) and put a hardwood border around the countertop. The hardwood borders, introduced in Scandinavia, are in style today and add elegance to a kitchen. Finally, remove as much grout as possible from the existing tiles and then regrout.

You can create a renovated tile countertop without actually replacing the tile! I have done this, and the results can be spectacular.

If the current tile countertop is not salvageable, consider an inexpensive Formica top. Although Formica and other laminates are not usually considered highly desirable by some homebuyers, they may serve well in a moderately priced home. Many large building-supply stores carry premade laminate tops, particularly in a butcher block design. These can be purchased in sections and quickly installed.

For a high-quality job, consider putting in new tile. Nothing speaks more of elegance in a kitchen. In a more expensive home, it will bring back more than the cost of having it installed.

Finally, for a fancy job, consider synthetic marble or another artificial surface. Keep in mind, however, that this requires expert installation and is quite expensive.

Cost

The cost of putting a hardwood border around existing tile and regrouting is basically the cost of the hardwood. Try using molding designed for use as a floorboard or a border around doors. It is readily available at lumber stores and is not expensive. The entire cost can be less than $50.

If you are going to go the premade Formica route, expect to spend several hundred dollars. Also, keep in mind that the Formica usually comes installed over pressed wood, which is very heavy. This means that you'll probably need a helper to get it home and do the installation. Don't forget to factor in the additional labor costs.

I would advise against installing Formica yourself. It seems as though it should be easy to do. However, less than a professional installation always seems to show in uneven seams and poor gluing. A professional can usually do it for less than $500.

If you're going to use tile and do it yourself, you have the cost of the tile, plus preparation of the surface, plus glue, grout and tools. The incidentals are less than $50. However, the tile can be quite expensive, beginning at about $1 per square foot. I suggest you get a modestly priced tile. Most buyers care only that the kitchen counters have tile that's not broken and dirty. Many won't really know the difference between tile that costs $5 per square foot and tile that costs $25 per square foot.

If you have a pro do it, there's not only the cost of the tile, but also the cost of the labor. Expect to pay between $1,500 and $3,500 for labor in the kitchen. Synthetic countertops such as Corelon are fabulously expensive. A low figure might be $2,500 with a higher figure near $7,000, depending on the size of the counter.

Installation and Degree of Difficulty

Wood Border. Remove the edge tiles and make sure the edge is flat. Cut and attach the wood borders, then seal the wood. Finally, regrout to the edge of the wood. The entire job can be done in a day and it requires little skill. Go slowly to avoid mistakes.

Premade Laminate. Measure precisely the length you need. You may need to shorten or lengthen the existing cabinets to accommodate the premade pieces. (Some stores will take your measurements and then cut the countertop to fit. This takes longer and may cost a bit more, but is well worth it.) Drill and screw the Formica top to the counters from below, using takeup bolts to hold sections together.

Use glue where possible. Very little skill is required here, apart from lifting heavy pieces.

Laminating your own surfaces requires special techniques. There are books available in bookstores that can help you.

Tile Countertops. For installing tile, see the section on tile in bathrooms in Chapter 6.

The hardest part of installing a tile countertop is probably the preparation of the counter. Unlike floors, which usually must only be scraped, or a wall, where a flat, dry surface will do, the countertop must be perfectly level.

Remove the existing countertop base and discard. You will probably use a heavy piece of plywood (3/4-inch) as the new base. Use shims between it and the cabinets beneath to get it as level as possible.

Some remodelers now simply apply tile adhesive to the plywood and then the tile. The problem with this technique is that the surface will never be absolutely level. In order to get a perfectly level surface, you must apply a layer of mortar to the plywood. Use a level and trowel to create a perfectly flat surface. For a truly professional job, set the tile right into the mortar. Alternatively, the mortar can be smoothed and allowed to dry, and then an adhesive used. (It takes weeks for the mortar to dry properly.)

The level of skill needed for installing counter tile is high. It is unlikely that you will get a good-looking job the first time, so if you can, practice first on an area such as an outdoor counter that doesn't matter too much.

Synthetics should be installed only by professionals.

What To Watch Out for When Installing

Wood Border. Be sure that there's no more room between the wood and the first layer of tile than between any other row of tiles. You may have to cut through the wood base of the counter to shorten the top in order to make the border fit. Also, be sure that there is a way to adequately anchor the wood border. Use brass screws if possible instead of nails, or the border may later separate from the counter. Be sure the wood border is no higher than the surrounding tiles. Be sure to stain the wood before you grout; if you don't, the acids in the grout will discolor it.

Premade Formica. Because you are working with existing cabinets, be sure that the new Formica top is wide enough to fit all the way over, allowing for several inches of overhang. Try not to cut the new countertop, ending up with an uneven line. If you do have to cut it, use an electric saw blade with very fine teeth. When you screw in the countertop, be sure your screws aren't too long, or they will protrude into the Formica, thereby lifting or even cracking it.

Tile. Getting the surface level is tricky. Use a very long level—eight feet or more. Getting the tile down in straight lines is also hard. Use of corner guides helps, but does not solve all the problems. Draw a guideline on the surface and set a first row up against it. Also, get down at eye level frequently and look up the rows as you place the tile. Your eye from countertop level is often far more accurate than any other measurement.

Be careful to observe the drying times for the materials you use. For adhesives with short drying times, do only a very small patch.

After you place each tile in the adhesive, be sure to tap it with the blunt end of a hammer or other tool. This helps it set and attach more strongly.

See the section on tiles and bathrooms for more hints.

Typical cost of materials	
Wood	$50–$75
Premade Formica	$250–$500
Ceramic tile	$1–$25 per sq. ft.
Synthetics	$2,500+
Time to complete	20 hours
Degree of difficulty	𝑇𝑇𝑇𝑇𝑇𝑇𝑇𝑇
Do-it-yourself/Hire someone	**DO IT** ~~HIRE OUT~~

■ RENOVATING CABINETS

■ *PROBLEM*

The cabinets are a kitchen's glory—or its shame. Fine wooden cabinets are indicative of an elegant home. Shoddy, painted cabinets with doors that don't close indicate a cheap house that needs work. If there's one area of the home that it pays to spend time and money on, it's the cabinets.

The trouble is that in most remodels, the kitchen cabinets are in terrible shape. The doors may be hung badly, scratched, discolored or even missing. The cabinets themselves may have been of cheap construction when new and, now that they are old and abused, they are simply worn out and wrecked. There may not be enough cabinets for the kitchen.

■ *SOLUTION*

There are at least four acceptable ways to fix kitchen cabinets.

1. Paint the cabinets and rehang the doors correctly. This usually involves at least scratching, if not stripping, the existing surface. It should be attempted only on good-quality kitchen cabinets. New hardware (handles) should be put on at the time.

2. Refinish the cabinets. This involves stripping the existing varnish or paint and then restaining them. This should be done only if the cabinets are made of a good-quality hardwood.

3. Re-cover the cabinets with new doors. This involves scratching the existing surfaces and then gluing on a thin veneer of stained hardwood, usually oak. New oak doors are also normally put on at this time, as is new hardware.

4. Purchase and install new cabinets. The old cabinets are then disassembled and lugged out. Often they are junked, although they may be reused in the garage or rec room. Brand-new cabinets are then installed. Note: If new cabinets are installed, you will also need to install a new countertop; see the preceding section.

Cost

The cost of painting existing cabinets is the cost of the paint, stripping material and sandpaper. All costs except for labor will probably be under $100.

Refinishing the cabinets requires using much more of the stripping chemicals, although the job is essentially the same as above, though with much more labor (materials cost perhaps $150).

Re-covering the cabinets involves getting special hardwood veneers and having new cabinet doors made to order. The cost for materials alone is probably $1,500 to $2,000 for an average-sized kitchen. Double that for the labor of having it all installed.

Installing new cabinets involves the cost of buying the cabinets. The prices vary widely. The cheapest complete kitchen will probably cost about $1,500. A deluxe kitchen can cost more than $10,000.

Installation and Degree of Difficulty

Anyone can scratch the existing cabinets and then repaint them. If you can sandpaper and paint, you can do the job. (Be sure to use one of the new acrylic higher-gloss paints that mimics the old oil-based paints. They are amazingly easy to put on, and cleanup afterward is a breeze.)

Refinishing requires working with strong stripping chemicals. The instructions with the chemicals are quite good and anyone can do the work. Some of the new chemicals actually dissolve the old finish and then reapply it! It can come out looking wonderful. If you haven't tried this sort of thing lately, look into the latest products.

Re-covering with new doors is strictly a job for professionals. I don't recommend that anyone but a woodworker attempt it. The level of skill required to make new doors to fit old cabinets is high.

Finally, there's the matter of installing new cabinets. Although it might appear that this is the most difficult job of all, it's actually the easiest. Once the old cabinets are removed, simply place the new cabinets where you want them to go. Usually they are abutted against one another or extra spacing boards are used. Then screw them to each other and the floor. It's less than one day's job for an entire kitchen! (Of course, then you have to install a countertop base and a countertop, which is a different story—see the preceding section.)

Ready-made cabinets are available by order (or sometimes in stock) from large hardware and building-supply stores.

What To Watch Out for When Installing

When scratching, you want to sandpaper only the surface so that the new paint will stick. If you go too deep you'll make grooves that will show through. Be sure you use a high-quality brush to paint, as the secret is in getting good brush strokes.

If you refinish, the exacting work is in getting off the old stain. You have to be sure that all of the wood ends up with the same amount of removal. Apply the new stain with a brush and then wipe with a cloth for more even stain.

When installing new cabinets, the key is in buying right. Measure carefully so you end up with the right kind of cabinets and the correct sizes. Ready-made cabinets usually come in standard sizes so you can more easily place them next to each other. Be sure to abut the fronts tightly and screw them together. Any spaces or crooked alignment will show in the finished product.

Typical cost of material	
Paint	$100
Refinish	$150
Resurface	$1,500–$3,500
New	$1,500+
Time to complete	
Paint	16 hours
Refinish	24 hours
Resurface	1 week
New	8 hours
Degree of difficulty	
Paint	T T
Refinish	T T T
Resurface	T T T T T T T T T
New	T T
Do-it-yourself / Hire out	
Paint	**DO IT** ~~HIRE OUT~~
Refinish	**DO IT** ~~HIRE OUT~~
Resurface	~~DO IT~~ **HIRE OUT**
New	**DO IT** ~~HIRE OUT~~

■ INSTALLING A NEW SINK

■ *PROBLEM*

The old sink is too small, discolored, cracked or otherwise ugly or old-fashioned. In short, it makes the kitchen look bad.

■ *SOLUTION*

You can either refinish the old sink (see the section in Chapter 6 on refinishing tubs) or replace it. If you decide to replace the kitchen sink, you probably will have to do some work to the countertop as well (though not necessarily, as we'll see shortly.) You may need to enlarge the opening to accommodate a large sink, although if you're not planning to redo the countertop, I suggest using a sink of the same size as a replacement.

Kitchen sinks come in two varieties. One fits snugly against the countertop base with tile laid right up to it, or in some cases over it. The other variety has a lip, and it fits over the surface of the counter. For reinstalling where you don't want to redo the entire counter, use the latter variety. If you do a careful job of removing the old sink, without damaging the counter too much, you can build up the counter where the old sink was with wood or mortar and then put the new sink right on top. If you buy one with a wide enough lip, the work you did won't show at all!

Cost

You can get a kitchen sink in metal or in porcelain over steel. The cheaper ones are available for less than $50. From there the price goes up. I have seen a kitchen sink selling for over $1,000. It's hard for me to imagine what benefits it would offer over a lower-priced one.

I suggest avoiding the cheapest sinks, as the porcelain is thin and may chip or wear away easily. Also, stay away from the cheapest stainless steel sinks. For some reason, they stain! A moderately priced sink, perhaps around $100, might fit the bill just right. Add another $50 for new faucets.

Installation and Degree of Difficulty

There isn't a lot of skill involved in installing a sink. You have to make sure it fits the cutout (hole). Sometimes it's easier to install the faucets before putting the sink in. (See the section in Chapter 6 on installing a bathroom sink.) A sink with a lip usually has tightening screws underneath that hold it firmly to the counter surface. A flush-mounting sink sometimes has a metal ring that the sink fits into from the bottom and then tightens up with screws. The entire installation, including hooking up the drain and faucets, shouldn't take more than a couple of hours.

What To Watch Out for When Installing

The biggest problem I have with sink installations is that I never seem to have all the parts I need on hand. I am always having to go back to the hardware store for a piece of tubing or some extra drain pipe.

If you plan ahead and cover all contingencies by buying extra parts (particularly for the drain) that can later be returned, you'll save yourself a lot of time and headache. There should be no exceptional problems when installing a sink, except that the sink is heavy and you must be careful not to drop it onto the counter while placing it.

Typical cost of materials	$150–$500
Time to complete	2 hours
Degree of difficulty	*TTT*
Do-it-yourself/Hire someone	**DO IT** ~~HIRE OUT~~

■ INSTALLING A GARBAGE DISPOSAL

■ *PROBLEM*

The house is old and there is no garbage disposal connected to the sink, or the existing garbage disposal does not work well.

Today, homebuyers expect to have a garbage disposal. It's not that this adds anything to the price of the home. It's just that if a unit is not there, the buyer will think something is wrong with the property. The absence of a garbage disposal in a modern home detracts from value. In other words, you simply must have one.

■ *SOLUTION*

Install a garbage disposal. These are readily available at any hardware store. Most units fit standard sinks and drains. If your drain is an unusual size, there are special adapters available in PVC pipe to solve the problem.

Cost

You can get a cheap garbage disposal on sale for as little as $25. However, the cheaper units tend to have smaller motors and quickly get clogged when any kind of tougher material (such as carrots or chicken bones) is sent down the drain. This could result in problems for you or complaints from your buyer.

I always go for at least a 1/2-horsepower unit. These typically cost between $50 and $75 on sale. This is usually sufficient to handle most items sent down the drain. I buy the cheapest 1/2-horsepower unit available. I avoid fancy-looking units, such as Sears used to sell, because appearance doesn't count. No one looks under the sink to rave over the appearance of a disposal. Buyers just want to be sure one is there.

Installation and Degree of Difficulty

It takes only about two hours to install a garbage disposal and the skill level is low. However, it is tricky and because you're working under the sink, you'll probably end up with bruised fingers and a couple of bangs on the head. (You may need a permit.)

You'll have to remove the existing drains under the sink and reroute with new drains. (Don't try reusing the old drain material. New PVC drains cost only a few dollars, and this avoids potential leaking problems common with old pipes.)

The new disposal includes a flange and mounting assembly with instructions. The disposal is inserted from the bottom and attaches to a ring that comes down through the hole in the sink. A snap ring holds it from the bottom.

Be sure to install a new trap (to prevent sewer gases from passing up into the house) and new couplings on all drain joints.

What To Watch Out for When Installing

To avoid any possibility of leaks, install a bead of plumber's putty under the top flange (the part that goes into the sink). Many disposal instructions don't mention this, but instead include a thin paper washer. Don't overlook the putty. It will prevent a lot of leaks later on.

From the bottom, the snap ring is usually held in place with three screws. You put it on, twist, then tighten the screws to securely mount the unit. Some disposals, however, have a twist ring that you must twist tight. You'll need a special, wide disposal wrench for this. It's inexpensive and sold in hardware stores.

Be sure the unit is securely in place; when it's turned on, it vibrates significantly. If it's loose, the vibrations can cause it to leak.

Typical cost of materials	$50–$75
Time to complete	2 hours
Degree of difficulty	$\mathcal{T}\mathcal{T}\mathcal{T}$
Do-it-yourself/Hire someone	**DO IT** ~~HIRE OUT~~

■ INSTALLING A DISHWASHER

■ *PROBLEM*

The home does not have a dishwasher or the present dish-washer doesn't work or looks bad. Old dishwashers often get rusted areas inside, especially on the dish racks.

■ *SOLUTION*

If the rust and ugly areas are just on the racks, try to get new racks. These are available for the more common models. It can be a quick-and-easy solution.

If the unit doesn't work properly but looks good, fix it. A professional can usually repair whatever ails the dishwasher for less than $100. If it has major operational problems and looks old-fashioned, or there are areas on the inner walls that have rusted, replace it. A buyer coming into the house will invariably open the dishwasher. If it looks bad inside, it will make the buyer cautious. He or she will wonder what else you've overlooked in your remodeling.

Cost

I have purchased Whirlpool or GE dishwashers on sale for as little as $250. Complete installation is often only $50 more plus installation parts (which run another $10 or $15). If you have the time, however, you can quickly install the unit yourself.

Installation and Degree of Difficulty

It takes virtually no skill to install a dishwasher. You have to be sure you have adequate room under the counter. Often, removing a cabinet will give you the space. The unit fits right under the counter-top and usually attaches to the countertop with two screws. In older units, there may be additional screws to hold it to the floor. Newer models have feet that adjust up an inch or so to help fitting.

You may need to install a tee in the hot-water pipe and a shutoff valve in order to supply water to the unit. The dishwasher needs only hot water, not cold. Also, you may need to install an electric outlet under the sink if one isn't already there.

Be sure that you include an overflow air gap, required by most building codes. This is a plastic device that comes up through a hole in the sink (if your sink has four holes, that's what the fourth one is for), screws on and has a chrome cap. Normally the outlet goes into the garbage disposal, but if the outlet is plugged, the water will drain out of this air gap into the sink.

Many municipalities require a building permit for the installation of a dishwasher.

What To Watch Out for When Installing

Be sure the unit is level so that it doesn't vibrate when turned on. Be sure all pipe fittings are tight so water leaks don't develop over time. Because the plumbing is under the sink, leaks might go undetected for quite a while, damaging or warping wood.

Typical cost of materials	$250–$600
Time to complete	1 hour
Degree of difficulty	$T\,T$
Do-it-yourself/Hire someone	**DO IT** ~~HIRE OUT~~

■ INSTALLING A NEW STOVE/OVEN

■ *PROBLEM*

The existing stove/oven is old or broken or it looks so old-fashioned as to make the kitchen unappealing.

■ *SOLUTION*

Throw out the old and install a new one. There is very little incentive to fix the old unit. The cost of new electric burners, for example, is prohibitively high. You can often buy a new range/oven for the cost of just two or three burners! Old gas units, on the other hand, sometimes plug up with grease. The cleaning job is messy, and if the valves are affected, cleanup is ineffective: It's simply easier to get a new unit.

Cost

There are a variety of stove/ovens. Drop-in range ovens can be purchased for about $300. Wall ovens are about the same price; however, you'll need to buy a separate drop-in cooktop for an additional $150 or so. Standalone units tend to be expensive, perhaps $350 and up as of this writing.

Installation and Degree of Difficulty

Installing a unit requires no skill and can be accomplished in a matter of minutes. What does take time and skill is creating the openings for them. With the exception of the standalone, you'll need to have cabinets that accommodate. The drop-ins are the most common. However, the side cabinets (which hold the unit in place) have critical spacing because the drop-ins are often held by only a half-inch of cabinet on each side. All units come with specific measurements, and you should obtain these measurements before installing new or rebuilding old cabinets to fit.

Electric units require a 220 volt outlet, which must be available nearby, typically hidden from view under the counter. Gas units use a flex pipe to connect to a gas outlet.

What To Watch Out for When Installing

Be sure that the drop-ins fit snugly and are screwed in tightly. You don't want them falling out the first time someone opens the oven door!

Be sure to get a permit if required in your area. If you're working with gas, you may be exposing yourself to great liability if something adverse should happen. It may be cheaper in the long run, with gas, to have a pro install the unit.

Typical cost of materials	$250–$500+
Time to complete	1–2 hours
Degree of difficulty	*T T T*
Do-it-yourself/Hire someone	**DO IT** ~~HIRE OUT~~

■ NEW LIGHTING FIXTURES

■ *PROBLEM*

There isn't enough light in the kitchen or the lighting is in the form of an old-fashioned fixture.

■ *SOLUTION*

Install new lighting. (See the section on lighting in Chapter 6.)

Modern kitchens have recessed lighting. Fluorescent lights are recessed six to eight inches into the ceiling in a large panel, often 4×8 feet. Translucent plastic sheeting covers the panel and is held in place by a stained wood frame. This design provides excellent lighting and also modernizes the kitchen.

You'll be able to do this only if you can find room in the ceiling to recess the light panel. Because most older homes don't have any room to recess a panel, the alternative solution is to drop the kitchen ceiling by six to eight inches everywhere except where the light fixture is. In short, you create a false ceiling to conceal the fixture. The dropped kitchen ceiling can be appealing by itself because it varies the look of the room.

As a simpler alternative, you can buy a boxed fluorescent fixture that fits right onto a ceiling surface. It simply plugs into the existing socket and is held on with screws. It isn't as nice as recessed lighting, but is much easier to install.

Cost

Fluorescent light fixtures (to be concealed) can be found for around $20 apiece, including bulbs. Boxed fluorescent light fixtures (to be exposed) usually begin at $75–$100. You may want to use two or more to adequately light the kitchen.

If you decide to remodel and create a recessed fixture, you will have not only the cost of materials, but also the time spent lowering or adjusting the ceiling. The cost will vary with each job.

Installation and Degree of Difficulty

A surface-mounted unit simply screws into studs. The wires connect to the box for the existing light fixture. The total installation time should be half an hour or less, with virtually no difficulty.

A recessed lighting fixture requires reconstruction of the kitchen ceiling. The degree of difficulty here is moderate. A building permit may be required. What's usually done is that 2" × 6" boards are nailed onto the existing ceiling studs, leaving an area for the recessed lighting. Then the studs are covered with wallboards, taped, textured and painted. This creates a lower ceiling with a recessed box.

Basic fluorescent lights are attached to the old ceiling inside the box. A wood frame is built for the bottom, with cutouts to accommodate translucent plastic sheeting, and the frame is then screwed or nailed into place. Finally, the fluorescent tubes and plastic sheets are put into place.

What To Watch Out for When Installing

For a recessed installation, be sure that the box and the frame are large enough to accommodate the fixtures and the translucent plastic sheeting. The sheeting may be cut, if necessary, to accommodate an awkward fit. The fluorescent lights, however, are more difficult to shrink. The lights usually come in four-foot lengths. Three- and two-foot lengths are available; however, the price for these is often twice as high.

Typical cost of materials	
Recessed	$250+
Surface	$200
Time to complete	
Recessed	10 hours
Surface	1 hour
Degree of difficulty	
Recessed	↑↑↑↑↑
Surface	↑
Do-it-yourself/Hire out	**DO IT** ~~HIRE OUT~~

■ NEW LINOLEUM FLOORING

■ *PROBLEM*

Existing flooring is worn, scratched, rotted or otherwise deteriorated so much that it's no longer useable or attractive.

■ *SOLUTION*

Install new linoleum flooring. The big advantage of linoleum over tile or hardwood is the ease of installation and reduced cost (although top-quality modern linoleum can be quite expensive). The appearance can be excellent. Modern linoleum wears well and you avoid the problem of slipping that can occur with tile floors. Although some people consider tile flooring the only truly deluxe way to handle a kitchen, many people actually prefer modern linoleum. I always use it instead of the far more expensive tile or hardwood alternatives.

Your choices are essentially between a single piece of linoleum and the many different types of linoleum squares.

Cost

Single-piece linoleum can cost from $5 to $35 per square yard (3' × 3'). Individual squares can cost as little as 50¢ per square foot or as much as $5 per square foot.

The big difference, however, is in the cost of installation. Professional installation of single-piece linoleum costs about $5 per square yard. Linoleum squares are roughly the same price. However, you can install them yourself much more reasonably.

Installation and Degree of Difficulty

The floor must be dry and sealed. A whole sheet of linoleum is then cut to fit counters, walls and corners. Then it is glued down.

The job requires great skill. The linoleum is often rigid and must be softened using a blow-torch. However, too much torching can easily burn it. Also, getting the proper cutouts is very difficult with a single large piece, as is making joints for larger areas. It is almost impossible for a first-timer to do an acceptable job. Professional installation is a must for sheet linoleum.

Individual squares, particularly those that come backed with glue, are easy to cut and lay down. A pair of scissors, cutting knife, pencil and cutting guide are all you need. Because you are working with a single small piece at a time, it is fairly easy to cut out areas to fit around cabinets, corners and walls. The skill level required is modest and most first-timers can do an acceptable job.

What To Watch Out for When Installing

With individual squares, be careful not to get the glue onto the top. It will attract dirt, discolor and become ugly. It's also fairly difficult to remove. Be sure the squares fit tightly but not too tightly. If they are forced into place under pressure, they will buckle.

Also, be sure to draw a starting line near the center of the floor and work out from it. If you start at one side of the room and work across, you may find that your lines are off by the time you reach the other side.

Typical cost of materials		
Sheet	$5+ per yard	
Squares	$0.50+ per ft.	
Time to complete		
Sheet	10 hours	
Squares	5 hours	
Degree of difficulty		
Sheet	𝚻𝚻𝚻𝚻𝚻𝚻𝚻𝚻𝚻𝚻	
Squares	𝚻𝚻	
Do-it-yourself/Hire someone		
Sheet	~~DO IT~~	**HIRE OUT**
Squares	**DO IT**	~~HIRE OUT~~

■ INSTALLING A SKYLIGHT

■ *PROBLEM*

There is not enough natural light in a kitchen (or other area of the home). Most people prefer to have natural light in kitchens. However, because of the location of the kitchen in the house (no outside walls) or because nearby buildings are close to the walls, it may be impossible to enlarge or add a window.

■ *SOLUTION*

Add a skylight. They are in style and attractive, and they add a lot of light without taking up any extra room. Of course, you have to be sure that it is indeed possible to add a skylight. You can't add one to a kitchen in a two-story house!

Cost

For a simple skylight added to a pitched roof with standard asphalt or wooden shingles (not a tile roof), the materials probably won't cost much over $350, including the plastic bubble. The labor involved is probably another $500 if you hire it out. However, you should be able to do it yourself in a relatively short time.

Installation and Degree of Difficulty

It is a multiple-part process. First you must cut the hole in the roof, frame it and cut a hole in the ceiling. Then you have to create a light shaft, using wallboard. Finally, you have to add the skylight bubble at the top.

The skill level is moderate and it can usually be done roughly in a day with the finish work completed in a second day.

What To Watch Out for When Installing

Do the work on a day when no rain is expected. You don't want to cut a hole in the roof just as it starts pouring.

Also, when you frame the roof cut, you want to be careful to avoid weakening the roof. This is particularly important in areas with snow-load requirements. The easiest way is to add the skylight between two existing beams. If the space between beams is too narrow, however, you'll have to cut one beam and frame a box. This could weaken the roof too much: You'll have to check with an engineer to be sure.

Be careful to add flashing up the edge of the skylight on the outside. This will help to ensure that the skylight doesn't leak in heavy rain.

Typical cost of materials	$350–$500
Time to complete	16 hours
Degree of difficulty	𝈀𝈀𝈀𝈀𝈀
Do-it-yourself/Hire someone	**DO IT** ~~HIRE OUT~~

Structural Remodeling

Sometimes a house will need some structural changes. Although these jobs seem most difficult, many are relatively easy to handle and can be done by a person with a basic knowledge of construction. As with Chapters 6 and 7, the purpose here is not to give a detailed explanation of how to do the work. We're trying to determine just what's involved, how hard it is, how much it will cost, whether an average person can do it, and what to watch out for.

■ HOUSE LEVELING

■ *PROBLEM*

The house is not level. One of the quickest ways to detect this is to take a marble and drop it in the center of a room where you suspect there is a problem. The marble should simply bounce around and lie near where it fell. If it rolls down toward one side of the room, you know you have a problem.

Unlevel houses are usually the result of soil problems. In some cases the soil expands, causing supports and foundations to rise unevenly. (Soil that expands when it gets wet is common in some parts of the country.) In other cases, supports and foundations may sink because of poor drainage or bad compaction of the soil before the house was built.

■ SOLUTION

This can be the most serious problem for a house. You would be wise to consider whether the problem is solvable before you buy. If it is not, you may want to pass on the purchase of the home.

The first step is correcting the underlying problem causing the slippage. When the problem is caused by poor drainage, a French drain could be installed around the house. This is porous pipe, usually four to six inches in diameter, installed in a bed of gravel, that drains water away from the house. Properly installed, a French drain should dry out soils under the house and stabilize expansion and contraction of soils.

When the problem is caused by slippage on a hillside, more radical steps may need to be taken. You may need to drive piles deeply enough into the soil to anchor the foundation. You may need to erect heavy cement blocking walls to keep soil from slipping down onto or out from underneath the house. You may have to increase the size of the foundation itself to anchor the house.

In the case of bad compaction of soil, as when the house was built on a lot that was cut and filled (dirt was cut out from a hillside and then used to fill the down slope), special cement/plastic compounds can be injected into the soil to reexpand and stabilize it.

With the exception of French drains, all of the other procedures are complex and should be undertaken only after you have consulted with an engineer. Also, keep in mind that the results are often unpredictable. The problem may or may not be corrected.

Generally speaking, these sorts of problems are peculiar to an entire area, not a single house. Often agents will be able to alert you to the problem even before you see the property. They may say something such as, "Houses in this area are all settling."

Once the problem has been solved, you can level the house. You may need to jack up the house and pour a new foundation. Depending on the severity of the problem, the house may be adjusted on the existing foundation. You might be able to jack up the house and cut the supporting beams that are too high, then lower the house back down onto them.

Cost

There is no way to guess the cost because each job is different. Call in an engineering firm for an estimate. Don't faint at the price. Typically, work of this sort is measured in tens of thousands of dollars.

Installation and Degree of Difficulty

Sometimes you can do it yourself, particularly in the case of installing French drains. Instructions for French drains are widely available. Most heavy corrective work, however, requires permits, approvals, engineering reports and professional help.

Here are two examples that may prove enlightening. I recently was asked to purchase a home built on a slab that, I was told, had slippage. I couldn't believe my eyes and sense of balance when I walked in. The house was perhaps 40 feet long and I was convinced that one end was four feet lower than the other! The house had been built on a cut-and-fill lot. The fill side had slipped out and the house had sunk.

The worst part was that it was on a slab. In order to correct the problem, the house had to be lifted off its peripheral foundation. The fill had to be compacted or solidified and built up. A new peripheral foundation and slab had to be poured and the house bolted back down. The estimated cost was $70,000!

Worse, it was a two-story house! The very process of jacking it up and then lowering it down might cause irreparable damage. Needless to say, I ran (not walked) away.

In another case, I bought a small single-story house that had a definite tilt to one side. The house was more than 40 years old, built on a raised foundation with wood floors.

An examination of the foundation revealed that one side had sunk a foot or more. Because there wasn't a drainage problem, I concluded that the slippage had resulted from compaction of the soil over a 40-year period. The question was what to do about it.

I decided that after 40 years the soil was probably as compact as it was going to get, so I left it alone. With some helpers, I used house jacks (similar to auto jacks, only hydraulic and capable of lifting enormous weight) to raise the sunken side of the house until it was above level. Then I inserted shims between the house and sunken foundation. The shims were simply thick pieces of redwood. Finally, I lowered the house back down to level.

I didn't need to rebuild the foundation because it wasn't badly cracked. I did rebolt the foundation to the house to make sure it wouldn't slip in the event of an earthquake or heavy winds. The total time involved was two days. The total cost, including helpers and materials, was less than $1,000. (In some areas, old floor beams will sag. A new permanent support in the basement will usually cure the problem.)

All of this says that you must be careful and selective. Some houses that aren't level are money pits. Others are real opportunities.

What To Watch Out for When Leveling

Don't get in over your head. This is one area where it pays to get expert estimates and help.

Typical cost of materials	$1,000+
Time to complete	10+ hours
Degree of difficulty	𝕋𝕋𝕋𝕋𝕋𝕋𝕋𝕋𝕋𝕋
Do-it-yourself/Hire someone	~~DO IT~~ **HIRE OUT**

■ ADDING A ROOM

■ *PROBLEM*

Sometimes a house is simply too small, or one area of a house may be too small. Typical problems include a house with only two bedrooms or a master bedroom that's too small, or one where the living area isn't adequate.

The problem of size means that you can't resell the house for enough money until it's expanded. With a house that's too small, no amount of renovating of the existing area will help. Lack of size only has one solution: expansion.

■ SOLUTION

Add or enlarge a room. The critical decision is where to add and how much. It's one thing to design a home from scratch. It's quite another to take a completed home and then design an addition that visually flows well, that makes sense, that complements the original house.

Too often, remodelers spend a great deal of time, effort and money on additions that end up looking awkward and that detract from rather than add to the property. My suggestion is that, every time, you get the services of an architect before you begin.

You may argue that an architect is very expensive. True. And not true. I'm not suggesting that you have an architect draw up a set of expensive plans. Rather, what I'm proposing is that you hire an architect to come down and take a look at your property. Have him or her tour it, then think about it and suggest where and what you should do.

A person who has the special skill of visualizing how a place will look before the work is done (an architect) can come up with solutions you may never have dreamt of. For example, you know that the master bedroom is too small. You had envisioned enlarging it by knocking out one wall into the back yard. But the architect suggests reducing the size of a closet in an adjoining room and moving a wall: a quicker, cheaper and easier solution.

Or you need to add living area, so you plan to expand the living room. But the architect suggests adding a totally separate family room on the side of the house. The cost is greater, but the results will look spectacular and bring a much higher price for the house. You may have to pay the architect for the advice, but in most cases you can draw up simple plans yourself or hire a draftsperson to do it for less than an architect would charge.

I have a friend who was once a commercial artist. He took that skill and talent and went into home renovation. He was able to walk through a home and sense what could be done to expand it cheaply and effectively. Today he has his own construction company specializing in renovations.

Cost

The only way to calculate cost here is on the basis of square footage. Generally speaking, the cost ranges from about $35 per square foot if you do the work yourself to about $150 if you have it done entirely by professionals. I encourage you to do as much as possible yourself.

Installation and Degree of Difficulty

The biggest problem with an addition is the mess. If you're attempting to live in the property while you do the work, you'll have outside walls covered only with plastic, which lets in cold and an occasional neighborhood dog or cat. You'll have dust everywhere. The noise of heavy construction will be with you most of the time.

To do the job you'll have to cut out a section of the existing house, then build out from scratch. This involves getting permits, putting in foundations, framing, roofing, doing electrical work and, perhaps, plumbing. Then there's finishing the interior with drywall, finishing the exterior, putting in windows and doors and, finally, painting. In short, it requires all the skills involved in building a house. Hence, the degree of difficulty is high.

Nevertheless, you probably can do most of it yourself. The first room addition I did, more than 15 years ago, took most of a summer. However, the only charge was for materials and an occasional helper. It turned out great and allowed me to resell the property for a significant profit.

What To Watch Out for When Adding

Plan on everything taking longer and costing more than you anticipate. Also, be aware that you will have to run the gamut of numerous building inspections. No matter how well you think you've done the work, the inspector is bound to find something wrong. Be prepared to rip it out and start over. Yelling at the inspector will only make things worse.

Typical cost of materials	$35+ per sq. ft.
Time to complete	Varies
Degree of difficulty	𝕋𝕋𝕋𝕋𝕋𝕋𝕋𝕋𝕋
Do-it-yourself/Hire someone	**DO IT** OR **HIRE OUT**

■ ADDING A GREENHOUSE WINDOW BOX

■ *PROBLEM*

A living room, family room or kitchen is dull and seems congested. You don't want to go through the expense of adding another room or expanding the current one. You want to liven up the area.

■ *SOLUTION*

Try adding a greenhouse window. They are currently all the rage. They extend the current window out away from the house about a foot and allow you to put plants in the extra space. They can also expand the size of the existing window.

Greenhouse windows are generally three to ten feet wide. because most standard windows are only three to five feet wide, going wider than five feet will mean making structural changes in the house.

Cost

The cost of the windows varies enormously, but a good aluminum frame with shatterproof glass can easily cost more than $350. The cost of installing it professionally varies with each job. You should get an estimate from a contractor who specializes in such installations.

Installation and Degree of Difficulty

It's not hard to install a simple greenhouse window, and you should be able to do it with a couple of days of work.

If the new window to be installed is the same size as the old, it's simply a matter of removing the old window and putting in the new. Along the way you will have to remove some of the exterior and interior finish (about four inches) around the window itself. You can use furring strips of wood to adapt the opening size to fit the new window. Then you'll have to refinish inside and out.

If the new window is larger than the old, you'll have to enlarge the opening. This means rebuilding the wall. You'll have to come up with a set of plans and probably get a permit. When you're ready to go, you have to remove the covering on the exterior and interior of the walls, cut out studs, and put in a new header board (the heavy board that goes across the top of the opening) before proceeding with the installation. You'll need to know basic construction techniques. This is much more difficult than installing a greenhouse window of the same size.

What To Watch Out for When Installing

Be sure to caulk all around the window and wrap building paper around the edges or use metal flashing to make sure there are no leaks.

Be sure to have help when lifting the window box into place. It's very heavy because of the glass and also quite easily broken.

If you're adding a larger window than exists, be careful not to disturb the diagonal braces in the existing wall. These are metal or wooden braces that run diagonally across the studs. They keep the house from falling over in an earthquake or heavy wind.

Also, be sure to install a header that is heavy enough. The building department can usually tell you the required size.

Typical cost of materials	$350+
Time to complete	40 hours
Degree of difficulty	⌐⌐⌐⌐⌐⌐⌐⌐⌐
Do-it-yourself/Hire someone	**DO IT** OR **HIRE OUT**

■ ADDING A FRONT DECK

■ *PROBLEM*

The front entrance to the house is poor. For example, it consists of two cement steps and a tiny entrance pad before the front door. It's small and old-fashioned and makes the house look cheap.

First impressions are always critical. A homebuyer will make a judgment, often from a first glance, at just how good the quality of a home is. If that first impression is bad, it will be very difficult to get that buyer to pay top dollar for the home. The poor entrance detracts from the home's appearance.

■ *SOLUTION*

Add a front deck. When we speak of decks, most people think of rear decks, a place to put the barbecue and spend leisurely afternoons.

Although that certainly is a good use for a deck, in most cases it does not pay to add a rear deck to a home. The cost of putting in the deck does not equal the increase in value it will give to the property. A front deck or porch, however, is a different story.

A front deck can transform an ordinary-looking house into something quite exquisite. It can give the house the zip it needs to make a great first impression.

Cost

The cost of a deck will vary depending on the size and the materials used. A good redwood or cedar ground-level deck can cost around $8–10 per square foot for materials. Elevated decks can cost substantially more. Cement decks can cost more or less depending on the situation. (This does not include the cost of labor.)

Installation and Degree of Difficulty

It's not hard to build a deck, but it usually takes time. Expect to take two or three days on an average deck.

It is beyond the scope of this book to give detailed instructions for how to construct a deck, but deck plans are readily available in a variety of magazines and books found in most bookstores. However, two experiences that I had in constructing front decks may prove enlightening.

The first deck was concrete. I purchased a house to remodel that had a small (4' × 6') entrance pad. Over the years it had cracked and one side tilted downward. It made the entire front of the house appear shabby.

I decided to put in a cement pad covering the entire front of the house, about 20 feet long by 10 feet wide. Although this was an expensive choice, I felt that it would add a kind of class to the front that couldn't otherwise be achieved.

I didn't bother to remove the old pad. Instead, I built a frame to hold the concrete and filled it with gravel, dirt and loose rock up to a height of about four inches from the top of the frame. I added mesh wire, so that the concrete would have strength, and had workers fill it with concrete. I then hired a finisher to smooth the surface and add tiny colored pebbles.

The result, to say the least, was spectacular. And not expensive. The workmen were doing it on their day off as a side project and charged only about $200. The entire job took three days. The level of skill required was just about nil except for the finishing of the concrete, which requires a high level of skill.

In another case, I added a heavy redwood deck to the front of another older home. This one had a similar entrance. There was no pad, but just three steps up. I added a 10′ × 12′ deck with three steps up running all around it. I simply put cement footings into the ground, added posts and crossbeams and then nailed in two-inch-thick boards.

This deck cost considerably more because the wood was more costly than the concrete. However, I did it all myself. It was like working with an erector set: putting the boards on top of each other in an orderly fashion. (Of course, there are formulas for the sizes of beams to be used and how they must be joined, and a building permit was required.) The level of skill was low.

This wooden entrance deck looked even classier than the cement entrance deck described earlier. I also added a mahogany door with cut glass, and the front of the house was a real eye-catcher.

What To Watch Out for When Installing

With a cement deck, be sure that the wire mesh or steel rods are in the concrete, not lying down under it. (If they lie down, they won't strengthen the cement.) Also, have a professional finisher work on the concrete, as it is a very high-skill job.

With a wood deck, be sure the top planks are not placed too close together, or when the wood gets wet and expands, it will swell and the deck will buckle. A good way to keep the spacing equal on the boards is to measure the distance between them by using a nail. As you butt up the boards, simply put a nail between them.

Typical cost of materials	$8+ per sq. ft.
Time to complete	24 hours
Degree of difficulty	
Cement	TTTTTTTTT
Wood	TTTT
Do-it-yourself/Hire someone	**DO IT** ~~HIRE OUT~~

■ ADDING AIR CONDITIONING OR NEW HEATING

■ *PROBLEM*

The heating system is broken, outdated or inadequate. In many older houses in the Southwest, for example, the heating system consists only of a couple of floor or wall furnaces. These are unattractive and make buyers think about the expense they will incur putting in a new heating system. Potential buyers may turn away, or they may subtract three or four times the cost of installing a heating system from the price they offer.

In some locales, air conditioning is necessary. This is increasingly the case, given its general popularity. Whether it's a "swamp cooler" or central air, air conditioning has become a necessity for getting a good price when selling a home in many areas, particularly for more expensive houses.

■ *SOLUTION*

Fix the existing system. Add central heating or air. Some older houses have gravity-fed, hot water, steam or oil-burning furnaces. If the existing furnace works, I always try cleaning it first. Sometimes a good cleaning is all that's needed. (It may be 40 years old and never have been cleaned!)

On the other hand, sometimes you just have to add or replace. The least expensive kind of central heating is forced air. Where natural gas is available, high-efficiency furnaces today are readily available for a minimal cost. Other types of heating, such as radiant hot water, can be substantially more expensive and don't warrant the cost in a remodel.

One thing you might consider is a wood-burning stove. These have become increasingly popular in colder climates and can be installed quickly and inexpensively, in most cases.

While installing central heating, consider getting central air. The additional cost, if done at the same time, can be much less than doing the two jobs separately. (Central air pays only in higher-priced homes in areas of very high temperatures or humidity.)

Cost

A high-efficiency 60,000 BTU, forced-air, natural gas furnace for a medium-sized house without duct work can cost about $1,200 installed. Add air conditioning for another $1,800 installed, minimum.

Installation and Degree of Difficulty

When it comes to installing any type of gas or oil-burning furnace, I always suggest having it professionally done. It's not that you or I couldn't do it. If something should go wrong, it may be disastrous. There could be a leak, an explosion or poison gas entering the house. If you plan to live in the house, you have the health of yourself and your family to consider. If you plan to sell or rent, you have liability exposure. If you have a professional do it, you're in much better shape, in terms of liability, than if you did it yourself.

Of course, what I'm talking about here is the furnace itself and the plenum (from which the ducts come out). The duct work, another major cost, is a different matter. In the old days, ducts were made of sheet metal and required strength and skill to form.

Today, ducts are made of flexible fiberglass ducting (a continuous wire coil wrapped with fiberglass and enclosed between two layers of plastic). Installing it is the essence of simplicity. Ready-made ducts are available at most building supply stores. In short, you can install the ductwork for an entire house yourself in a single day!

Air conditioning installation does not involve liability problems, does require some skill. Precharged units with precharged hosing are available, but I always have a pro do it. It's simply easier.

What To Watch Out for When Installing

If you're going to do the ductwork and have a pro install the furnace and air conditioning, be sure that you're clear on the size requirements. Think of it as if it were a tree. The furnace/air conditioner is the trunk. The ducts are the branches, and, like tree branches, they are thicker at the base and thinner as they extend out. Be sure to have your furnace/air conditioner installer who makes the plenum specify the thickness required for the ducting.

Typical cost of materials		
Central heat	$1,200	
Central air	$1,800+	
Time to complete	24 hours	
Degree of difficulty		
Ducts	$\int \int$	
Do-it-yourself/Hire someone		
Central air	~~DO IT~~	**HIRE OUT**
Central heat	~~DO IT~~	**HIRE OUT**
Ducts	**DO IT**	~~HIRE OUT~~

These, then, are a few of the structural changes you may want to make on a remodeling project. No matter what you do, however, keep in mind that structural changes are the hardest, most time-consuming and, usually, most expensive. They may certainly be necessary in order to make the house more attractive and saleable, but they may also be avoidable. Check your calculations many times to see if there isn't some cosmetic correcting you can do before considering a structural change.

Furthermore, keep in mind that everyone's skill level is different. A difficult job for me might be an easy one for you. In the above jobs, the assumption is that you have average abilities and levels of skill. You will have to adjust the degree of difficulty upward or downward to meet your specific needs.

■ ═══ CHAPTER 9 ═══ ■

Landscaping—Getting Better Curb Appeal

First impressions are critical, and the most critical impression is the one made when a potential buyer, drives up to the home. This is called curb appeal.

This first impression can be greatly enhanced by the external appearance of the property. New paint and a good-looking front door are important, and landscaping in the front is critical. If there's one area in which money spent will more than double the return, it's front landscaping. (One old agent I knew used to repeat to me, "You can't sell a house with a brown lawn in front.")

The questions, of course, concern what kind of front landscaping and how much should you do. That's what we'll deal with in this chapter. Note: Side-yard or back-yard landscaping is nice, but basically it is unimportant. You can simply turn over the dirt and leave it bare in the side and back yards and get away with that. It won't enhance the house, but it won't terribly detract from it either. On the other hand, front-yard landscaping is absolutely critical.

■ LAWNS

I believe that every house needs a front lawn. Even in the drought-ridden Southwest (where I'm from), I always put in a front lawn.

Of course, the lawn doesn't have to be big. Even a 10' x 20' patch is enough. In fact, a small front lawn is often more appealing than a large one because it suggests less yard work to a potential buyer. To put in a small lawn, pick a patch of level dirt in the front, put in underground sprinklers (a necessity for a lawn in dry areas), cultivate the soil, add fertilizer, spread some seed around and add covering. In a month you'll have a reasonably good lawn, good enough to help land a buyer.

Avoid Expensive Lawns

The lawn described above can be started as soon as you get the property. In dry areas, install the underground sprinklers right away and plan the lawn so that it'll grow while you remodel the property. When you're done with the house, the lawn will be ready.

I always stay away from turf and instead plant seed. Although turf gives a better lawn, its real advantage is speed: You can have a growing lawn in an afternoon with turf. However, as described above, speed isn't a problem, so why go to the expense? (I recently put in a lawn for the cost of a box of seed—about $15, not counting the sprinklers. Turf would have cost $1,000!)

Mow and Water

A well-manicured lawn attracts buyers—one that hasn't been mowed or is starting to turn brown drives them away. Be sure to keep the lawn well trimmed and watered.

■ TREES, BUSHES AND HEDGES

Trees and shrubs are nice and add a feeling of maturity to the property. However, planting them costs a bundle. I rarely plant trees, bushes and hedges. However, almost all properties I have bought already have them, though often in a terrible state.

As soon as I get the property I begin watering the trees, bushes and hedges. It's hard to overwater them. If they've been neglected for a long time, it may take them a month or more to come back. It may already be too late for others and they may die.

Anyhow, after a month, I have a good idea what's going to make it and what's not. Then I begin trimming. It may well be that I'll have to remove a tree or bush to increase the beauty of the front yard, but mostly it's a matter of trimming things back so that they look neat and presentable. Next, I add fertilizer and watch them take off.

Note: I don't believe in adding fertilizer to a neglected plant. My experience is that if the plant is far gone, the fertilizer may push it over the edge. Rather, I just water and see what happens. Once the plant starts recovering, the fertilizer gives it a boost. On the other hand, if it dies, I've saved myself some extra cost in fertilization that I didn't do.

■ FLOWERS

Of course, working with just the existing trees, hedges and bushes usually results in some bare spots and some holes in the front landscaping. These I fill with brightly colored flowers. Depending on the season, they are readily available from gardening stores at minimal prices.

They can be planted in a cultivated bed soon after you buy the property. Often, all that's needed is water and a tiny bit of fertilizer. They will bloom and within a month the front of your house will look like a magnificent garden.

Don't underestimate the value of flowers in front. Even if they're in pots, they add greenery and color and brighten an otherwise dull house so much that people turn their heads as they go by.

If there's one area that you spend your money on, let it be flowers for the front. Nothing will give you a bigger return on your investment when remodeling!

■ THE FIRST TASK

Unfortunately, for many remodelers, front-yard landscaping is the last item considered. Countless hours of time are spent renovating the home. Money is poured into the structure. The front yard remains neglected until everything else is done. Then, some minimal front yard work is done.

Don't make the mistake of not valuing the front yard. The first task when you buy a property to remodel should be to get the front yard and lawn into shape. It will take only a day or two of work. Then it will grow while you do the actual remodeling. Work with your front yard and garden and it will work hard to make your home a quick, high-priced seller.

■ ══ C H A P T E R   1 0 ══ ■

Buying a Fixer-Upper

Everybody who's into remodeling has heard of a fixer-upper. It's a run-down house that you can buy for a lower price. You then rehabilitate it and, hopefully, resell for a profit. The goal of many remodelers is to eventually take on this big, full-house rehab project.

■ MAKING A PROFIT

When working with a fixer-upper, the important thing to remember is that you make your profit when you buy, not when you sell. If your goal is to buy a fixer and rehab it, then the key to your success is buying right. That means getting an appropriate property at the right price.

After you've been at it for a while, you'll develop a kind of sixth sense that will alert you when the property and the price are right. Even so, whether it's your first deal or your fiftieth, it pays to take it one step at a time. The analysis you do before you buy is the most critical.

In this chapter we're going to see how to find a good deal, recognize it, and get it for a good price. If you can accomplish these seemingly difficult tasks, you're more than halfway through a successful full house remodeling project.

How do you recognize a good remodeling deal? Examine each property you come across and check it out against the three cardinal rules of total home remodeling.

RULES FOR TOTAL HOUSE REMODELING (REHABBING)

- Be sure the work is within your abilities.
- Be sure it's a good location.
- Get the right price.

■ STAY WITHIN YOUR ABILITIES

The first reason to rule out a property is that the work required to remodel it is far beyond your abilities. Regardless of how well-priced the home may seem or how good the location, are the problems so onerous that you just can't handle them?

Let's take an example. Recently I was looking at a home in a very high-priced neighborhood where comparable houses were in the $500,000 range. The house I was considering was the subject of a great deal of interest by a variety of remodelers because it was priced at $350,000. The house itself was in good shape. The problem was that it was on a steep hillside and the foundation underneath had given way. It was supported by matchsticks—a few piers in the ground at the bottom of the hill with boards reaching up 20 feet were all that held it in place. I was actually afraid of walking on the rear deck for fear that it might collapse.

I offered $300,000 subject to an inspection (a contingency) by someone who knew foundations and soil better than I. The offer was accepted.

On the surface I had a terrific deal—a $200,000 margin to play with. It seemed that I could easily fix what was wrong for that price and still sell at the market price for that neighborhood, turning a healthy profit.

Not so—it turned out that the reason the foundation had collapsed was water runoff. The house was built near an old creek bed. During heavy rains, water as much as 15 feet below ground poured out from under the house. To stabilize it, a dozen steel and cement piers would have to be sunk 25 feet into the ground. Even then the results were speculative. The house might not be savable.

I exercised the contingency clause and escaped from the deal. Maybe someone with experience in hydraulics and earth movement could handle it, but the problem was far beyond my expertise.

You will find similar "bargains." They may not involve the foundation or the earth. They could involve structural damage, roof damage or kitchen and bath repairs. You may realize that the work that needs to be done is more than you know how to handle. If that's the case, my advice is to stay away. Although you might learn as you go and succeed, more likely you will end up wasting a lot of money and perhaps even losing the property. Stay away from deals that are over your head.

■ FIND A GOOD LOCATION

Unfortunately, many properties that are suitable for home remodeling may turn out to be in run-down sections of the city. In fact, if you go to any blighted area of any major city, you will find hundreds, probably thousands, of homes that are candidates for total home remodeling (and their price is usually quite low). The problem is that even though they might be cheap and within your abilities to remodel, you won't be able to make a profit, perhaps not even get your money out when it comes time to sell, because of their poor location. Later on, you'll find that no one wants to buy your "dream home."

Whether you're considering buying or already own, let location be a determining factor. It may turn out that the house that you have is simply not suited to remodeling because of where it's located.

Do Good Homes That Are Run Down Exist in Great Neighborhoods?

Yes, they do, but finding one can be difficult. The problem is that very often the sellers of such homes will do the remodeling work themselves if there isn't too much involved. This means that your chances of finding one at a good price that needs only paint and wallpaper is remote.

Most sellers understand buyers. They realize that the majority of buyers who can afford to purchase a home in a good neighborhood don't want to buy a house that is run-down and is going to require a lot of fixing up. These buyers want to move into a home that's ready to go. Consequently, if all that it takes to get the house into shape is some cosmetic work—painting, recarpeting and a bit of landscaping—the current owner will usually do the work and then sell at full price (the price for which other homes in good condition in the neighborhood are selling).

On the other hand, if it's going to cost a lot of money to remodel the property (more than $10,000 or $15,000), the current owner will often despair of the cost (and time) of fixing up the property and will sell it as-is.

That's where you come in. You want to find a house in a good neighborhood that has problems too big for the current owner to remedy easily. You can then offer a low price and have a reasonably good chance of getting it.

Keep in mind that most homes such as those we've just described tend to be in older neighborhoods (at least 20 years old). Although it's possible to find a problem house in a new neighborhood, it's unlikely, unless the problems are so severe that they scare even you away!

WHAT TO LOOK FOR

- Houses with problems that exceed $10,000 to fix

- A bad home in a good neighborhood

- Usually an older neighborhood

Sources To Help You Find the Right House

Where can you find just the right house? Almost anywhere. You have to go looking. Suitable houses are almost always available. You have at least three separate sources for information on them:

1. Real estate brokers

2. Sign in front of house

3. Advertisements in local newspapers

Let's consider each separately.

Brokers. Almost everyone who wants to sell a house uses a broker. This does not mean, however, that any broker or only one broker will do. Some brokers, particularly when they have what they think is a great property, will refuse to cobroker. Others may simply not be very competent and may not know what's on the market.

I've had the best results by making friends with a very active broker, one who lists and sells a lot of properties. This kind of broker, anxious for a sale, usually is willing to work closely with me and allow me to look at the *Multiple Listing Service (MLS)* book, which lists all the homes for sale. (Note that most MLS organizations state that the broker is not allowed to lend the listing book to clients or, in some cases, even to let them see it. Many brokers, however, are willing to stretch these seemingly over-restrictive rules.) Most MLS books contain pictures of most of the listings as well as descriptions of the properties.

This is where you need to do your homework. You need to go through the book (with the agent) looking for the following:

WHAT TO LOOK FOR IN THE LISTING BOOK

- Homes for which the price seems low for the neighborhood
- Homes that have been on the market a long time
- Homes that show disrepair

Check out the pictures in the listing book, but remember that problems don't always show on the outside. One big hint is a bad roof. Missing shingles or stains on the roof may suggest problems. Look also at the paint. Although the photo is in black and white, paint discolorations, peeling, or cracking of stucco or brick surfaces are often visible.

Also look at the landscaping. Often a run-down house will have run-down landscaping. If the lawn is shown in the picture, is it well-mown or is the grass long? Are the shrubs neat and trim? What about the fences—are they leaning over or upright with no missing boards? Often the landscaping can be your best clue as to the actual condition of the property.

Check the listing broker's comments. All listings include information on the size of the home, number of bedrooms and baths and so forth. They also leave a fairly large area for the broker's comments. Check these carefully. Look for the following or similar words:

- Opportunity

- Challenge

- Fixer

- Needs TLC (tender loving care)

Brokers are brilliant at understating problems. They will do their best to say a negative in a positive fashion. I've never seen a listing in which the broker said, "This is a dog and only a remodeler would like it!" Rather, they couch their comments in terms that suggest what opportunities the property might offer to just the right person (you?). Anytime you see any of the above words or similar ones, you may have found your remodeling project.

For Sale by Owner (FSBO). Sometimes owners want to avoid paying the sales commission and instead try to sell the house on their own. This can be a good opportunity for you, but don't expect them to be great deals every time or even most of the time. Occasionally, you may find a gem.

Advertisements. Finally there's the matter of advertisements in local newspapers. Get into the habit of checking them daily. A broker who doesn't have a property listed in the MLS may advertise. An FSBO that you have not seen may be listed there. This is also an excellent source.

GET A GOOD PRICE

It's important to understand the difference between buying a home to live in and buying a remodel. With a home, if you love it, you may be willing to pay more than you at first considered offering. Remodeling, on the other hand, is strictly business.

It's also important to remember that whether a price is too high is a relative thing. Too high for whom? Certainly no price is too high for the seller. The question becomes, Is the price too high for you, fair though it may seem to the seller?

FORMULA FOR DETERMINING THE RIGHT PRICE

Purchase price + Cost of rehabbing + Profit =
Resale price (less costs of sale)

The formula simply says that the price you pay for a property plus the total costs of home remodeling plus your anticipated return must equal what you can resell the property for after costs of selling (such as commission and closing costs).

Unfortunately, applying the formula is a bit more difficult than simply learning it. To apply the formula, you must determine three things in advance and then work backward:

1. The total costs of home remodeling

2. The profit you want

3. The future resale price

Let's consider each element separately.

Determining the Total Cost of Remodeling

You must be able to take a close look at the project and see what work needs to be done and what can be overlooked. You must also determine what you will do yourself and what you will hire out. Then you must come up with a figure that has to be pretty close to actual costs.

Of course, you will get better at this over time. Initially, however, you may need to call in tradespeople to ask their advice and to get bids from them. A quick word of advice: When you're just starting and need to call in other tradespeople for estimates, lock in the deal first.

Lock in the deal first.

If it's a really good deal, chances are that there will be other remodelers out there looking to do what you're doing. They may be more experienced and able to make estimates on their own. For example, while you're trying to get a roofer to look at the property, one of these other more experienced remodelers may estimate the costs and then buy the property before you do.

One way around this is the contingency offer. You offer to buy the property and make the purchase contingent on an inspection within a specified period of time. Most sellers won't object, provided that the time for the inspection is short (seven days is typical). Once the seller agrees, call out the people you need to look at the property and find out exactly what your costs are going to be. They are not competition because you've locked in the deal.

The plan is not perfect. The problem is that you might offer too much or too little. You won't know the correct price until after you make the offer, and by then it may be too late. If you offered too much, you have only two alternatives. You can try to renegotiate the price with the seller. (Bringing a very unfavorable inspection report to the seller's attention can sometimes succeed here. After all, the seller is going to run into the problem no matter who buys, and a buyer in the hand is worth 20 lookers.) Your other alternative is to walk away.

The contingency offer is a way to try to get a good deal when you aren't sure of your estimating abilities. It's not the best answer. The best answer is to be a good estimator of costs.

Determine Your Profit

How much do you want or need to make on the deal? Note that I'm speaking here of the remodeler who plans to resell relatively soon for a profit. If you're planning to renovate and live in the property indefinitely, calculating profit isn't critical. You may still want to go through the exercise, however, to be sure you don't overspend.

There are many ways to calculate this. Perhaps the best I've seen is to apportion an hourly rate for the time you spend home remodeling (also see Chapter 5). Then, add return on investment amount on top of that.

HOW TO CALCULATE YOUR PROFIT

Hourly wage + Return = Profit

Some remodelers will simply take a percentage of the total cost of the remodeling work or of the total cost of the property and figure that as their profit. A lot depends on your situation with regard to other work.

For example, let's say that you're a carpenter by trade. With the market in your area being down, you haven't had much work lately. Your goal is extra income. You might calculate the total number of hours you'll spend working on the job and then multiply that by your working hourly wage. On top of that you might add 5 percent, and that's your anticipated profit. That's what will make you happy.

Or you may be an investor. Your calculation could be very different. You will want to calculate an hourly wage for your time spent, but on top of that you'll want to add a significant return percentage to account for your risk on the deal as well as your return on money actually invested. You may want to add 25 percent. Some investors totally overlook the hourly cost and simply add a percentage, often 25 to 35 percent of the purchase price, when calculating what they want to get back on the project.

There is another consideration to be made with regard to profit: whether the house is low, moderate or high in price. Simply put:

> The higher the price of the house, the bigger your profits on your remodeling project will be.

The reasoning here is quite simple. Let's say your profit is 10 percent of the sale price. If the house sells for $100,000, your profit is $10,000. But if the house sells for $1,000,000, your profit is $100,000.

The amount of work required to remodel a more expensive house is usually not much greater than that required for a cheaper one. The difference in sale price usually can be attributed more to land value and neighborhood than to the house itself. It is for this reason that professional remodelers tend to work with the more expensively priced homes and avoid the lower-priced ones.

Unfortunately, there is a downside to this approach. In a bad real estate market, such as during the late 1980s and early 1990s, the higher-priced homes are the hardest to sell. For example, in the San Francisco Bay area during that period, any home priced under $250,000 in a good area was instantly sold. Any home priced over $300,000 couldn't be moved no matter how good a deal it was. (The San Francisco Bay area is one of the highest-priced—if not *the* highest-priced—housing areas in the country.)

I advise sticking to higher-priced homes when the market is good. Move to moderate-priced homes when it is bad. Stay away from low-priced homes at any time. (Not enough profit can be made there.)

Determine the Resale Price

This calculation, perhaps the most important, requires you to calculate how much the property will be worth after you finish the home remodeling.

Do NOT add up:

The cost of remodeling + Your return + Purchase price
and then assume that this will equal what the property
is worth when you are finished.

The ultimate sales price is determined by what comparable homes in the neighborhood are selling for. For example, let's say houses in good shape in the neighborhood are selling for $200,000. You buy a fixer-upper for $175,000 and put another $50,000 into home remodeling it. Is your property now worth $225,000?

No, it's still only worth $200,000. The reason is simple. Any potential buyer can choose between your house at $225,000 and a comparable one at $200,000. Which do you think the buyer will select?

The determination of final sales price has to be made without
consideration of the costs of home remodeling.

You can make this determination easily before you buy. Simply ignore the house that you are considering and find out what the other neighborhood houses of similar size in good shape are selling for.

That price, not your costs of home remodeling, is what you'll ultimately be able to resell for.

Don't Overlook Costs of Reselling

One area that many total home remodelers new to the field overlook is the cost of selling. Unless you sell by owner, often a difficult task, you'll need to take into account a commission to a real estate agent (usually 5 to 7 percent of the sale price) plus your closing costs.

I've seen some remodelers who have assumed that price appreciation will take care of these costs. They figure that it will be six months to a year before they sell and by then the property will have gone up enough in value to pay sales costs.

Unfortunately, in most parts of the country, real estate appreciation has been static or even negative for several years. It's a mistake to count on price appreciation to pay for your sales costs. (For help on selling your property, I suggest my books *Tips and Traps When Selling a Home*, McGraw-Hill, 1990, and *How To Sell Your Home in a Down Market*, Warner Books, 1991.)

Remember to work backward! You don't start with the sales price, then add on the remodeling work, profit and other costs. You start with the resale price, then subtract the costs of home remodeling and other expenses to determine the price you should pay.

■ MAKING AN OFFER

Once you've got the price you want to pay, you have to make a decision. Do you simply offer your maximum price, take it or leave it? Or do you offer a bit less, anticipating that the seller will counter and you can then come up?

To my way of thinking, it's six of one, half a dozen of another. Sticking to one figure and not budging will convince a seller that that's all you're going to pay. But it may also anger the seller and cause him or her to refuse to accept your price. Coming in low and then raising your offer to the maximum may console the seller, but may convince him or her that you'll be willing to go even higher in price.

You have to make the call yourself. Regardless of how you do it, however, chances are that you will offer far less than the seller is asking. After all, to make a profit with a remodeling, you often have to pay 25 to 50 percent below market cost for other homes in the neighborhood. Not too many sellers are going to be willing to do that, even for a fixer-upper.

What this means is that most of the time, you won't get the deal. Most sellers will refuse your offer as too low. Most of the time the seller will counter with an offer that is higher than your maximum.

Walking Away

When the seller counters higher and refuses to come down, you have no alternative. You have to walk away. You must never pay more than the maximum amount that you have calculated as affordable to pay for the property.

This is one rule that is set in stone. When you remodel a home, you're operating a business. The profits you make in your business are determined in large part by how adroit you are at buying right. Buy properties at the right price and the profits are there. Pay too much and you lose.

It's important not to get sentimental when the seller won't budge. Don't say to yourself, "That's the perfect remodeling project. Okay, I'll pay $5,000 or $10,000 more and take less profit." Don't do it. Don't fall in love with the house and allow your emotional attachment to sway you from your predetermined maximum price. To do so simply means that you'll lose money, and losing money is not your goal.

Make Lots of Offers

What all this means is that you're not likely to be able to buy many houses. Most of the time your offers will be rejected by sellers. Perhaps nine out of ten offers you make will be rejected and you'll come away empty-handed. Don't be discouraged. You're not in a high-volume business. Most full home remodelers (rehabbers) do only one house at a time, perhaps only one or two a year.

You don't need a lot of properties. What you need is the right property. It's better that you lose ten or even a hundred offers than you buy one property for too much money.

The problem with making a lot of offers, however, is that eventually most people begin to get discouraged. They begin to feel that it's impossible to get a house to rehabilitate. Don't give up hope. Make the search for the right property a hobby. You don't have to do it full-time. Just a few hours a week are enough. Keep checking with brokers. Drive around neighborhoods and check out FSBOs. Every day spend the few minutes it takes to look at the classifieds.

After you've done this for a month or so, you'll discover that you've become an expert. You'll begin to know neighborhoods and property values. You'll come to recognize where you want to buy a home and how much you'll be able to sell it for. No one can teach you this—it's part of your education in the field. Learning the market and making offers that don't go through is not wasting time. It's time spent educating yourself.

Ultimately you will find the right property and will know it's right because of all the properties you visited and all the offers that didn't work.

The right property will come along. Be patient.

Appraising for Remodelers

As I noted in Chapter 10, the way to make a profit in total home remodeling (also called *rehabbing*) is to be sure that the price you pay for the property plus the cost plus your profit is no more than the resale price (including costs of sale, such as commission). The formula taken from the previous chapter is:

FORMULA FOR DETERMINING THE RIGHT PRICE

Purchase price + Rehabbing cost + Profit = Resale price (less costs of sale)

The formula simply says that the price you pay for a property plus the total costs of home remodeling plus your anticipated profit must equal what you can resell the property for after costs of selling (such as commission and closing costs).

The quickest way to lose money is to pay too much. The problem, of course, is that you don't know how much to pay until you've determined what your ultimate resale price will be. (Remember that to determine how much you pay, you have to first determine your ultimate resale price, then work backward.)

Unless you can accurately determine the resale value of the property, you haven't a chance of being successful. In this chapter we're going to see how to appraise the future value of a property. It's not a difficult process or even a time-consuming one, but it is very important.

■ THE APPRAISAL PROCESS

All people in real estate know (or think they know) how to appraise a property. Here, we're going to take it one step further. Not only are we going to appraise a property, but we're going to appraise it in terms of what it will look like three to six months (or more) down the road, after we've completed remodeling. In other words, here we don't even have a finished product to appraise!

There are many techniques used in appraisal. For example, for income properties the rents are multiplied by a variety of figures to give prices. For other investment properties a return on investment or a capitalization figure is used. Sometimes for construction a building-cost figure is used to determine value. Although all of these procedures have their place, for us they are irrelevant. If you've heard of them before, put them out of your mind. For appraising a total home remodel, there is a unique procedure that I advocate. I call it projective appraisal.

Projective Appraisal

The term *projective appraisal* means that we are projecting our appraisal into the future. There are five steps:

PROJECTIVE APPRAISAL STEPS

1. Determine neighborhood maxi/mini values.

2. Compare size/shape/improvements.

3. Factor in trends.

4. Determine quality of renovation.

5. Give appraised value.

This five-step process should give a fairly accurate appraisal of your property value after total home remodeling. Let's take it one step at a time.

Determine Neighborhood Maxi/Mini Values

The essence of residential appraisal is comparison. Find a comparable property that has recently sold and substitute yours for it. If they are a match, then presumably the buyer of the other property would have just as easily bought yours if yours had been available. Comparables tell the story.

In conventional appraising, the real estate agent or appraiser or the buyer or seller checks sales of comparable properties over the past six months. This usually tells what the property in question is worth. For example, if three sales of comparable homes were for $150,000, $145,000 and $155,000, then it's a pretty good guess that our property should sell for around $150,000. The comparison of comparables is the method loan appraisers use to determine value. It's what assessors use. It is the most accepted method in the field and, although it is not without problems, it tends to give the best and most accurate values.

Our problem, however, is in finding finished comparables. How can we compare our property as it will look in six months (or whenever we finish remodeling it) when we're making the appraisal today? (Remember, we need to know that future value in order to determine how much we can afford to pay.)

The answer is that we look for finished properties, preferably those with similar neighborhood locations and floor plans.

It's a mistake to appraise the property in its current condition. The biggest mistake you can make when remodeling is to do a comparable appraisal on the property as it now stands. Presumably it is run-down, with significant problems. If there is a similarly run-down house in the neighborhood that recently sold as-is, you might be tempted to compare it to get an estimate of the subject property's current value. As noted, that would be a mistake.

The current value of the property can be determined only by working backward from a projective appraisal. What a comparable house in as-is condition sold for is irrelevant to you. Remember—what you're trying to determine is not what someone else might pay for the property as it now stands, but what you can afford to pay given the remodeling you want to do. It may turn out that what you can afford to pay is too low, given what other comparables have sold for as-is. Or it may be less than the seller wants to receive. If that's the case, then you need to move on to a different property.

The whole purpose of projective appraisal is to determine the price you should pay in order to make a profit. It's strictly business.

Find the Maxi and Mini Houses. As noted earlier, the biggest problem is in finding finished comparables. Ideally, what we need is to find an identical house in the same neighborhood that has been totally remodeled and then resold. That price is as close to the projected appraisal as we can get.

Finding such a property, however, is very unlikely in most circumstances, so we need to look for next best. Next best, in this case, is finding the maxi and the mini.

The maxi is the maximum amount that any comparable house in good condition sold for in the neighborhood in the past three years. This establishes your "most" figure, the most you're likely to get for your total home remodel no matter what you do to it. The mini represents the minimum that any comparable house in good condition sold for in the neighborhood in the past three years. This establishes your "least" figure, the least you're likely to get for your total home remodel, as long as you fix it up at least minimally.

Check with Brokers. To find the mini and maxi prices, check with local real estate brokers. The local MLS usually keeps track of resales, although going back more than a year may be a problem. Some computerized services can pull out sale prices at the touch of a few buttons. Brokers are usually more than willing to give you this information because it may mean a listing to them later on.

Visit the Properties. Once you find the mini and the maxi, get their addresses and visit the properties. At the least, you can see them from the outside. I'm never hesitant to knock on the door and explain my situation. I might say, "I'm going to be remodeling a property down the street and I'm looking for ideas. I was wondering what's been done to your house." I always dress presentably and, if there's a concern about crime in the area, I might even have a neighbor I already know or an agent come with me. Nine times out of ten I get invited in.

Compare Size, Shape and Improvements

Once inside, I can look for ideas and, more important, judge the size, condition and improvements of the mini or the maxi. In short, I can see how it compares with my property (or the one I'm considering buying). I might also get some clues about any special circumstances that affected the sales price: Did the buyer just fall in love with the property? Were there some special financing considerations that made a higher (or lower) price possible? Is the house truly unique?

The easiest things to compare are rooms. How many bedrooms and baths do the mini/maxi comparables have? What about living room, dining room, family/rec rooms? Other rooms? A quick tour of the house or just a couple of questions can tell you how comparable to your house the property is.

Judging actual size is more difficult. By walking through, you may be able to get a feel for the size of the home. However, the real determination of size is square footage. How big is the comparable? Most owners don't know the square footage of their homes. They may be off by hundreds of square feet.

I usually bring a 100-foot tape measure with me and ask if I can measure the comparable property. I do it on the outside, going around the periphery. It takes only a few minutes and almost no one objects. I do the same for the property I am buying (or considering buying), and I immediately have a very accurate size comparison.

How nice are the comparable mini and maxi? Are they in great shape with everything modernized, with good wallpaper and paint, with no problems?

This is a judgment call, and what I'm trying to do is see what a house like the one I'm buying should look like when finished. I probably will get some new ideas and dismiss some old ones. In any event, I should be able to get a feeling for what brings a good price and what doesn't.

Finally, there's the matter of improvement. Perhaps the maxi has an added bedroom or bath. Perhaps skylights have been put in. Maybe it has been completely modernized. On the other hand, maybe the mini-priced home remains just as it was built. (Maybe not. Maybe even the mini has been improved, indicating that just to sell in the neighborhood certain minimum improvements are necessary.)

A quick walk-through should tell us what the current and former owners have done to improve the property. Asking the current owner what he or she likes most about the house may also give clues about which improvements are more valued and which are incidental. In short, our goal here is to determine just how much work we will need to do to get the maxi price and to avoid the mini price when we resell.

Once you've seen the mini and the maxi, use common sense to determine which you want your total home remodel to most closely resemble. You may want it to be just like the maxi, but because of floorplan or square footage, you may be limited to having it come out like the mini.

Having made a judgment concerning which house yours will most resemble, calculate a comparable price. For example, if the maxi sold for $250,000 and the mini for $200,000 and yours will end up looking better than the mini but not nearly as good as the maxi, maybe your price based on comparables should be $225,000.

Of course, keep in mind that you're making a judgment on the basis of only two comparables, albeit perhaps the most important two. For more accuracy, try to see other properties as your time and patience allow.

Examine Trends

I've suggested that you look at comparables from the previous three years. However, most lenders, when they make appraisals for the purpose of giving mortgages, won't accept comparables more than six months old. Why go back three years? My purpose in considering older comparables is to get a true feeling for the maximum and the minimum performance of the neighborhood. Once that's established, I can then factor in trends.

For example, during most of the 1980s real estate prices in most areas of the country increased. However, starting in about 1987 and continuing through 1991, prices in many locales declined.

How did the neighborhood in which your property is located fare? Let's say your maximum-priced house sold for $200,000 two years ago. Prices have declined since then about 10 percent. When you factor in the trend, you now have to figure that the house is worth $180,000. Or let's say that prices have gone up 5 percent in the last year and your mini-priced home sold for $100,000 a year ago. Its current value is probably $105,000.

Of course, you're not simply interested in today's value because you won't be selling your home for quite a while, perhaps six months or more. What you really want to do is establish a price in the future.

This becomes a guessing game. What do you think real estate prices in the subject neighborhood are going to do during the time frame you have in mind: Go up, go down or stay constant? You can talk with brokers and with other investors and total home remodelers in the area. You can read the local papers, which often give clues about the market in their real estate sections. You can check with lenders.

But when all is said and done, no one knows the future, and your guess is as good as anyone's. My own feeling is that if prices are currently declining and there seems to be no end to the decline, I would seriously consider not rehabbing. The potential difficulties in reselling or in getting the right price are too great.

On the other hand, if the market has turned around and is stable or increasing, I'd go ahead. I'd be very careful, however, to be conservative when factoring in any increase. At most I'd include a 5 percent increase in value over the next year in a particularly strong market.

If the market is dropping, consider staying away from total home remodeling. Get in only if it's stable or increasing in value.

Determine the Quality of Renovation

Looking at comparables should help you decide how much you want to do and at what level of quality. Concentrate on making a quick decision as to what you're going to do.

After having actually seen other properties in the neighborhood, you may want to go back to your estimate sheet and increase or decrease work, time and costs.

Whatever you do, keep in mind that buyers don't purchase exclusively by neighborhood, although location is certainly the single most important factor. Rather, when it comes to remodeling and renovation, there is room for experimentation. Maybe there's a way to expand a living room or add a sun room or do something else to the house that no one in that neighborhood has thought of, but that either you've seen done elsewhere or you have an original idea for. If it's not too costly and not too drastic, my suggestion is that you give it a try. You may be able to increase your resale value, and your profits, by being a trendsetter.

Establish an Appraised Value

You've found maxi/mini comparables in the neighborhood. You've gone to those houses (and perhaps a few others) to compare size, shape and improvements. Then you've factored in real estate trends for the area. Finally, you've added or subtracted because of the quality of renovation that's been done.

The result will be your projected appraisal, your best guess about how much the property will sell for when you get finished.

The projected appraisal is what you'll use to help determine how much you should pay to buy the property (working backward). Remember, from the projected appraisal value, you subtract the cost of the home remodel, the profit and the costs of sale to end up with the maximum price you can afford to pay for the house.

■ COSTS OF SALE

A few words need to be said about what it costs to sell property these days. The simple way of putting it is that it costs plenty.

Unless the market is too hot to touch, you'll need an agent. Also, there will be closing costs. Figure 11.1 shows some of the costs you can expect to pay. (Also, don't forget that there could be state and local income taxes to pay on any profits you make—see Chapter 13 on taxes.)

FIGURE 11.1 ■ Typical Closing Costs on a Resale

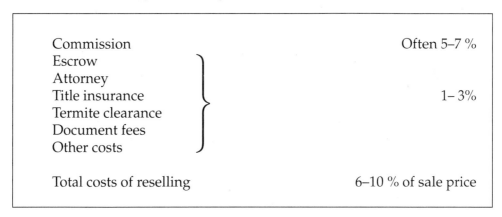

Commission	Often 5–7 %
Escrow	
Attorney	
Title insurance	1– 3%
Termite clearance	
Document fees	
Other costs	
Total costs of reselling	6–10 % of sale price

■ APPRAISAL CHECKLISTS

The checklists in Figures 11.2 and 11.3 should help you make an accurate appraisal of the property. They are designed to be used on maxi and mini comparable properties. Make copies of them to use when you want to appraise additional properties. To use the checklists, add or subtract dollars from the known sale price of the maxi or mini property, depending on whether the features of the comparable home are better or worse than the features of the home you're buying when finished. Remember, you're dealing in estimates, so try to be as conservative as possible.

FIGURE 11.2 ■ Comparing the Prospective Home to a Maxi Home

General

Sale price: $ _____

Sale date: _____

Address: _____

_____

_____

Owner's name:

Exterior

Location: Corner lot___   Center lot ___   Key lot ___   Busy street ___

Slow street ___   Cul de sac ___   Electrical above ground ___

Below ground ___

Better than your property—Subtract $ ___

Worse than your property—Add $ ___

Neighborhood: Residential ___   Mixed with commercial ___

Houses of similar design ___   Houses of similar age ___

Messy neighbors ___   Nearby industry ___   Air pollution problems ___

Noise problems ___   Vandalism ___

Better than your property—Subtract $ ___

Worse than your property—Add $ ___

Lot: Lot size ___ × ___   Regular ___   Pie-shaped ___

Irregular shape ___

Better than your property—Subtract $ ___

Worse than your property—Add $ ___

Landscaping, Front

Lawn ___   Clean ___   Neat ___   Trimmed ___   Messy ___

Overgrown ___

FIGURE 11.2   *(continued)*

Shrubs ___   Clean ___   Neat ___   Trimmed ___   Messy ___
Overgrown ___

Mature trees ___   Clean ___   Neat ___   Trimmed ___   Messy ___
Overgrown ___

Flower beds ___   Clean ___   Neat ___   Trimmed ___   Messy ___
Overgrown ___

Hedge ___   Clean ___   Neat ___   Trimmed ___   Messy ___
Overgrown ___

Ivy ___   Clean ___   Neat ___   Trimmed ___   Messy ___
Overgrown ___

Waterfall ___   Deck ___   Stonework ___   Brickwork ___

Pathway ___   Cement ___   Stone ___   Other ___   Neat ___   Broken ___

Better than your property—Subtract $ ___

Worse than your property—Add $ ___

House Front Exterior

Curb appeal: Strong ___   Average ___   Weak ___

Roof: Wood shingle ___   Cracked ___   Missing ___

Asphalt shingle ___   Curled ___   Missing ___   Discolored ___

Tile ___   Cracked ___   Missing ___   Broken ___

Tar & gravel ___   Patches ___   Other type ___

Siding: Clapboard ___   Shingle ___   Brick ___   Stucco ___

Aluminum ___   Stone ___   Other ___

Okay ___   Cracking ___   Rotted ___   Dented ___   Some missing ___

Crooked ___   Peeling ___   Loose ___

Windows: Large ___   Small ___   Bay ___   French ___

Shutters ___   Screens ___   Storm windows ___

FIGURE 11.2   *(continued)*

Paint: Okay ___   Color ___   Cracked and peeling ___

   Faded ___   Discolored ___

Chimney: Front ___   Side ___   Brick ___   Other ___   Painted ___

Special treatment to front: _____

                                        Better than your property—Subtract $ ___

                                        Worse than your property—Add $ ___

Entrance

Porch ___   Overhang ___   Separate entry ___   Cement ___   Tiled ___

Front door: Plain wood ___   Hardwood ___   Carved ___

   Glass insert ___   Gold handles ___   Double ___   Needs paint ___

Light: Common ___   Ornate ___   Hanging ___

Mailbox: Common ___   Covered ___   Elaborate ___

                                        Better than your property—Subtract $ ___

                                        Worse than your property—Add $ ___

Interior

Living/Dining/Family rooms

Color scheme: _____

Portals: Doors # ___   Openings # ___   Other ___

Windows: Large ___   Window seats # ___   Window gardens ___

Ceiling: Type ___   Discolored ___   Cracked ___   Peeling ___

   Water-stained ___

Walls: Paint ___   Wallpaper ___   Water-stained ___

Fireplace: Stone ___   Brick ___   Other ___   Discolored ___

   Broken ___   Smoke damage ___

Floors: Hardwood ___   Ceramic tile ___   Marble ___   Slate ___

   Other tile ___   Linoleum ___   Problems ___

FIGURE 11.2   *(continued)*

Carpeted ___   Plush ___   Shag ___   Multilevel ___

New ___   Worn ___   Color ___   Problems ___

Stairway: Hardwood ___   Ceramic tile ___   Marble ___

Slate ___   Other tile ___   Linoleum ___   Problems ___

Carpeted ___   Plush ___   Shag ___   Multilevel ___

New ___   Worn ___   Color ___   Problems ___

Closet ___

Light fixture: Special ___   None ___   Standard ___

Special features: _____

Better than your property—Subtract $ ___

Worse than your property—Add $ ___

Kitchen

Appearance: Painted ___   Wallpaper ___   Tile ___

Other ___   Problems ___

Floors: Wood ___   Carpet ___   Linoleum ___   Ceramic tile ___

Marble ___   Slate ___   Other tile ___   Problems ___

Cabinets: Standard ___   Old-fashioned ___   Refinished ___

New ___   Problems ___

Counters and sink: Ceramic ___   Formica ___   Wood ___

Other ___   Problems ___

Appliances: Stove ___   Oven ___   Gas ___   Electric ___

Dishwasher ___   Compactor ___   Garbage disposal ___

Light fixtures: Incandescent ___   Fluorescent ___

Special features: _____

Better than your property—Subtract $ ___

Worse than your property—Add $ ___

FIGURE 11.2   *(continued)*

Baths

　Main ___   Guest ___   Master ___

　Large ___   Small ___   Problems ___

　Bath ___   Shower ___   Sink # ___

Cabinets: Standard ___   Old-fashioned ___   Refinished ___

　New ___   Problems ___

Counters and sink: Ceramic ___   Formica ___   Wood ___

　Other ___   Problems ___

　Special features: _____

　　　　　　　　　　　Better than your property—Subtract $ ___

　　　　　　　　　　　Worse than your property—Add $ ___

Bedrooms

Number ___   Master ___   Bath in master ___

Size: ___ × ___,   ___ × ___,   ___ × ___

Windows: Large ___   Window seats # ___   Window gardens ___

Ceiling: Type _____   Discolored ___

　Cracked ___   Peeling ___   Water-stained ___

Walls: Paint ___   Wallpaper ___   Water-stained ___

Garage: One-car ___   Two-car ___   Three-car ___

　Condition: _____

　Special features: _____

Attic: Finished ___   Insulated ___

　Special features: _____

Basement: Finished ___   Insulated ___

Special features: _____

FIGURE 11.2 *(continued)*

Washer/Dryer: In-house ___   In-garage ___   Outside ___

Plumbing: Galvanized steel ___   Copper ___

Heating: Peripheral ___   Central ___   Gas ___   Hot water ___

Oil ___   Electric ___   Solar ___   Wood-burning ___

Special features: _____

Better than your property—Subtract $ _____

Worse than your property—Add $ _____

Total subtracted	$ _____
Total added	$ _____
Market trend factor	× ____ percent
Quality factor	× ____ percent
Adjusted sale price	$ _____

MARKET TREND FACTOR

The sale price plus or minus the cost of features is what you can expect a house like yours to sell for either at the maximum or the minimum, depending on the comparable you are examining. You should now factor in an adjustment for the market trend, upward or downward:

Market trend factor × ____ percent

QUALITY FACTOR

If the work you're going to do on your property is going to be better or worse than that on the comparable, you should factor this in as well:

Quality factor × ____ percent

FIGURE 11.2   *(continued)*

Note: Almost all of the terms used in these appraisal checklists are self-explanatory, but a few are not:

Key lot: a lot next to the corner lot that has the back of two other lots facing it

Curb appeal: the first impression a buyer forms as he or she drives up

Portals: passageways between rooms of a house

FIGURE 11.3 ■ Comparing the Prospective Home to a Mini Home

General

Sale price: $ _____

Sale date: _____

Address: _____

_____

_____

Owner's name   _____

Exterior

Location: Corner lot___   Center lot ___   Key lot ___

Busy street ___   Slow street ___   Cul de sac ___

Electrical above ground ___   Below ground ___

Better than your property—Subtract $ ___

Worse than your property—Add $ ___

Neighborhood: Residential ___   Mixed with commercial ___

Houses of similar design ___   Houses of similar age ___

Messy neighbors ___   Nearby industry ___

Air pollution problems ___   Noise problems ___   Vandalism ___

Better than your property—Subtract $ ___

Worse than your property—Add $ ___

Lot: Lot size ___ × ___

Regular ___   Pie-shaped ___   Irregular shape ___

Better than your property—Subtract $ ___

Worse than your property—Add $ ___

Landscaping, Front

Lawn ___   Clean ___   Neat ___   Trimmed ___   Messy ___

Overgrown ___

FIGURE 11.3   *(continued)*

Shrubs ___   Clean ___   Neat ___   Trimmed ___   Messy ___
   Overgrown ___
Mature trees ___   Clean ___   Neat ___   Trimmed ___   Messy ___
   Overgrown ___
Flower beds ___   Clean ___   Neat ___   Trimmed ___   Messy ___
   Overgrown ___
Hedge ___   Clean ___   Neat ___   Trimmed ___   Messy ___
   Overgrown ___
Ivy ___   Clean ___   Neat ___   Trimmed ___   Messy ___
   Overgrown ___
Waterfall ___   Deck ___   Stonework ___   Brickwork ___
Pathway ___   Cement ___   Stone ___   Other ___   Neat ___
   Broken ___

                          Better than your property—Subtract $ ___
                          Worse than your property—Add $ ___

House Front Exterior

Curb appeal: Strong ___   Average ___   Weak ___
Roof: Wood shingle ___   Cracked ___   Missing ___
   Asphalt shingle ___   Curled ___   Missing ___   Discolored ___
   Tile ___   Cracked ___   Missing ___   Broken ___
   Tar & gravel ___   Patches ___   Other type ___
Siding: Clapboard ___   Shingle ___   Brick ___   Stucco ___
   Aluminum ___   Stone ___   Other ___
   Okay ___   Cracking ___   Rotted ___   Dented ___
   Some missing ___   Crooked ___   Peeling ___   Loose ___

FIGURE 11.3 *(continued)*

Windows: Large ___   Small ___   Bay ___   French ___

   Shutters ___   Screens ___

Paint: Okay ___   Color ___   Cracked and peeling ___

   Faded ___   Discolored ___

Chimney: Front ___   Side ___   Brick ___   Other ___

   Painted ___

Special treatment to front: _____

_____

                        Better than your property—Subtract $ ___

                        Worse than your property—Add $ ___

Entrance

Porch ___   Overhang ___   Separate entry ___   Cement ___   Tiled ___

Front door: Plain wood ___   Hardwood ___   Carved ___

   Glass insert ___   Gold handles ___   Double ___   Needs paint ___

Light: Common ___   Ornate ___   Hanging ___

Mailbox: Common ___   Covered ___   Elaborate ___

                        Better than your property—Subtract $ ___

                        Worse than your property—Add $ ___

Interior

Living/Dining/Family rooms

Color scheme: _____

Portals: Doors # ___   Openings # ___   Other ___

Windows: Large ___   Window seats # ___   Window gardens ___

Ceiling: Type ___   Discolored ___

   Cracked ___   Peeling ___   Water-stained ___

FIGURE 11.3   *(continued)*

Walls: Paint ___   Wallpaper ___   Water-stained ___

Fireplace: Stone ___   Brick ___   Other ___   Discolored ___

   Broken ___   Smoke damage ___

Floors: Hardwood ___   Ceramic tile ___   Marble ___   Slate ___

   Other tile ___   Linoleum ___   Problems ___

   Carpeted ___   Plush ___   Shag ___   Multilevel ___

   New ___   Worn ___   Color ___   Problems ___

Stairway: Hardwood ___   Ceramic tile ___   Marble ___

   Slate ___   Other tile ___   Linoleum ___   Problems ___

   Carpeted ___   Plush ___   Shag ___   Multilevel ___

   New ___   Worn ___   Color ___   Problems ___

   Closet ___

Light fixture: Special ___   None ___   Standard ___

Special features: _____

                     Better than your property—Subtract $ ___

                     Worse than your property—Add $ ___

Kitchen

Appearance: Painted ___   Wallpaper ___   Tile ___   Other ___

   Problems ___

Floors: Wood ___   Carpet ___   Linoleum ___   Ceramic tile ___

   Marble ___   Slate ___   Other tile ___   Problems ___

Cabinets: Standard ___   Old-fashioned ___   Refinished ___

   New ___   Problems ___

Counters and sink: Ceramic ___   Formica ___   Wood ___

   Other ___   Problems ___

FIGURE 11.3   *(continued)*

Appliances: Stove ___   Oven ___   Gas ___   Electric ___

   Dishwasher ___   Compactor ___   Garbage disposal ___

Light fixtures: Incandescent ___   Fluorescent ___

Special features: _____

                                 Better than your property—Subtract $ ___

                                 Worse than your property—Add $ ___

Baths

   Main ___   Guest ___   Master ___

   Large ___   Small ___   Problems ___

   Bath ___   Shower ___   Sink # ___

Cabinets: Standard ___   Old-fashioned ___   Refinished ___

   New ___   Problems ___

Counters and sink: Ceramic ___   Formica ___   Wood ___

   Other ___   Problems ___

   Special features: _____ ___

                                 Better than your property—Subtract $ ___

                                 Worse than your property—Add $ ___

Bedrooms

Number ___   Master ___   Bath in master ___

Size: ___ × ___,   ___ × ___,   ___ × ___

Windows: Large ___   Window seats # ___

   Window gardens ___

Ceiling: Type ___   Discolored ___

   Cracked ___   Peeling ___   Water-stained ___

Walls: Paint ___   Wallpaper ___   Water-stained ___

FIGURE 11.3   *(continued)*

Garage: One-car ___   Two-car ___   Three-car ___

   Condition _____

   Special features: _____

Attic: Finished ___   Insulated ___

   Special features: _____

Basement: Finished ___   Insulated ___

Special features: _____

Washer/Dryer: In-house ___   In-garage ___   Outside ___

Plumbing: Galvanized steel ___   Copper ___

Heating: Peripheral ___   Central ___   Gas ___   Hot water ___

   Oil ___   Electric ___   Solar ___   Wood-burning ___

Special features: _____

   Better than your property—Subtract $ ___

   Worse than your property—Add $ ___

Total subtracted	$ _____
Total added	$ _____
Market trend factor	× _____ percent
Quality factor	× _____ percent
Adjusted sale price	$ _____

MARKET TREND FACTOR

The sale price plus or minus the cost of features is what you can expect a house like yours to sell for either at the maximum or the minimum, depending on the comparable you are examining. You should now factor in an adjustment for the market trend, upward or downward:

Market trend factor × _____ percent

FIGURE 11.3 *(continued)*

QUALITY FACTOR

If the work you're going to do on your property is going to be better or worse than that on the comparable, you should factor this in as well:

Quality factor × _____ percent

Note: Almost all of the terms used in these appraisal checklists are self-explanatory, but a few are not:

Key lot: a lot next to the corner lot that has the back of two other lots facing it

Curb appeal: the first impression a buyer forms as he or she drives up

Portals: passageways between rooms of a house

For additional help in appraising, I suggest two other books: *Tips and Traps When Selling Your Home* (McGraw-Hill, 1990) and *Buy, Rent, and Hold* (McGraw-Hill, 1991), both by my favorite author.

■ ═ C H A P T E R 1 2 ═ ■

Financing for Remodelers

In this chapter we're going to look at only one kind of financing: that which is advantageous to remodelers. Here, we're covering the financing you may need to buy a property for a total home remodel as well as the financing you may need to cover smaller remodeling jobs. Let's cover loans for the small job first.

■ REMODELING LOANS

There are a wide variety of home improvement mortgages available from banks, savings and loan associations and credit unions. They are of two types.

Home Equity Loans

The most common is the equity mortgage. Here, the lender offers you a certain percentage of your equity in the property, usually in the form of a second mortgage. The problem with this type of equity loan for remodelers occurs when you don't have much equity in your home. Typically this occurs if you recently bought and put only 10 or 20 percent down. That means that your purchase-money-first mortgage will be for 80 or 90 percent of the current value of the property (not the value after you've improved it).

Most home equity loans, however, are for a combined loan-to-value ratio of 80 percent. Thus, not having enough equity after the purchase, you may not qualify for one of these easy-to-get loans. (They are easy to get because the lender doesn't care what you do with the money. You can spend it on a holiday spree in Hawaii as far as the lender is concerned!)

Another alternative is a true home improvement mortgage. These are offered by the same lenders (some as FHA loans), but they are a bit harder to get and they cost more. True home improvement loans are based on the value of the property after the improvement is made and are usually paid out in installments as the improvements go in. You don't need any existing equity for these. They are much like a construction loan.

Home Improvement Loans

The qualifications for these loans are tougher, and you often must show either that you have a competent builder who is going to do the work or that you are competent (as proven by past experience or training) to do the job. You fill out a full mortgage application and you must carefully describe all the work you plan to do. You must also submit an appraisal from a qualified appraiser (usually specified by the lender) stating the value of the property after all the improvement work is done.

Finally, if you, the property, and the work to be done qualify, you'll normally get your money in installments, dribbled out as the work gets done. If you sense that I don't think this is the most wonderful of all possible loans, you're right. However, if you need to get a loan, it may be the only way you can go.

Other Options

Of course, there are other types of loans available. There are always credit cards. You can pay for a remodeling job with plastic. But if you do and if you plan to repay over time, at least make sure that you get a low-interest credit card. In the current highly competitive credit market, many institutions offer interest rates half of what the highest rates are.

You can also apply for a noncollateralized loan. Many banks are offering these now as an alternative to a credit card loan. They usually offer lower interest rates and, as a consequence, lower payments.

Finally, you might be able to borrow from relatives. If you do, make sure you have a specific repayment schedule and follow it closely, or you could make a close enemy.

■ TOTAL HOME REMODELING LOANS

This is usually a totally different kind of loan. Here you not only want to get a loan to pay for the remodeling work, but you also need a mortgage with which to buy the property. Before we get into loan specifics, let's consider an important aspect of this type of financing—whether you're going to live in the property or whether you're going to just buy and quickly resell. (It makes a BIG difference.)

The Owner-Occupied Advantage

There are two kinds of total home remodelers: the person who does it full-time as a business and the one who does it part-time as a hobby. Interestingly enough, financing favors the part-timer, the hobbyist.

The reason has to do with occupancy. The person who remodels full-time rarely occupies the house being worked on. He or she buys a property, or several properties, and then works swiftly getting the house(s) into shape for resale as soon as possible.

The part-timer, on the other hand, typically lives in the house being remodeled, whether it's a small one room remodel or a total house rehab. Lenders like this part-timer; they don't like the full-time remodeler. The reason is that they don't like people who buy and sell real estate as a business. They feel that this business is inherently risky. What if you get in over your head? What if the market turns sour and you can't sell the house when planned? What if you run out of money halfway through and can't make the mortgage payments?

All of these problems are risks to a lender, risks that could result in having to foreclose and take the property back. And no lender wants a half-remodeled property—it can't easily be resold and it requires the lender's attention to fix it up. Thus, lenders instinctively distance themselves from anyone who comes to them with what is essentially a small business proposition—remodeling a house.

Further, retail lenders (those who give you mortgages) sell most of their loans to wholesale lenders (secondary market). The secondary market heavily favors owner-occupants.

Nonoccupant Loan

A full-time remodeler who doesn't occupy the property will have to get a nonoccupant mortgage. These are available (though decreasingly so), but the interest rate is higher and the costs of obtaining them (points) are also higher than for an owner-occupant mortgage. For example, the non–owner-occupant mortgage might be 1.5 points higher than the owner-occupant mortgage (a point is equal to 1 percent of the loan amount; 1 point on a $100,000 mortgage equals $1,000).

Furthermore, even though an owner-occupant might get a mortgage of up to 95 percent of the value of the property, a non–owner-occupant might be able to get a mortgage for only 75 or 80 percent of the value. This means that the non–owner-occupant might have to put significantly more cash into the property as a down payment.

All of which is to say that when you remodel part-time and live in the property, you have an enormous advantage when it comes to financing. Owner-occupied means significant cost savings.

By the way, don't even think about lying to a lender about being an occupant. Those who do set themselves up for fraud charges. The federal government investigates such cases and in recent years has prosecuted to the full extent of the law.

In short, I advise that, if at all possible, you should move in. The financing makes it a great way to go. Although the lifestyle may be a bit awkward (with construction going on around you), it can pay off big dividends. Quite a large number of families I know supplement their income by doing this. A few do it as their main income source.

Those who buy to live in and remodel usually purchase a home every two years. (You can defer the profits if you sell your principal residence and then buy another, meeting certain constraints, but no more than one house every two years. See Chapter 13 on taxes and remodeling.) They live in and fix up the property, then sell it. Typically the home they occupy is far bigger and more expensive than they could otherwise afford, which offers yet another reason to try this plan!

What About When the Property Is Uninhabitable?

Sometimes, the house is falling down a hillside or has a leaking roof or another problem that keeps you from moving in. In other words, the house is uninhabitable.

That shouldn't daunt you when it comes to getting an owner-occupant mortgage. If a lender is willing to make a loan on the property at all (remember, the loans are initially made on the property's current condition), then that lender will understand that you can't move right in, but first have to do corrective work. It might be a month or even four months before you move in.

The key is intent. If you honestly intend to move in, you're entitled to the benefits of an owner-occupant mortgage. The lender will certainly be aware of the problems and you can point out, in writing, that you intend to fix up the property to the point where it's inhabitable before you move in.

■ SOURCES OF MORTGAGE FINANCING

Almost any source that lends money on real estate is suitable. You can try the following:

- Banks
- Savings and loans
- Mortgage brokers
- Commercial credit companies
- Credit unions

The procedures are all essentially the same. You fill out an application. A standard credit report is obtained. You provide documentation of your income and bank balances. The property is appraised. If every-thing checks out, you get the mortgage. If it doesn't, you look elsewhere.

■ THE BEST LOANS FOR HOME REMODELING

Unlike the old days, there are hundreds of different kinds of mort-gages available today. Checking with lenders, in fact, can be terribly confusing as they glibly mention this loan and that. However, if you can remember that the two big types of loans are the fixed-rate mort-gage and the adjustable-rate mortgage (ARM), you're halfway there.

Be sure you understand the difference. With a fixed-rate mortgage, your interest rate is fixed for the life of the loan. If it's a 30-year loan, the rate doesn't change for 30 years.

With an ARM, the rate fluctuates. It goes up and down depending on economic conditions. It is always tied to an index, such as the aver-age cost of Treasury bills, and always has a margin above that index. Nevertheless, the important thing to remember about an ARM is that the interest rate changes over the term of the mortgage. There are hun-dreds of different kinds of ARMs.

For most people, I always recommend a fixed-rate mortgage. The reason is simple. With the fixed rate, you know where you stand at all times. You know what your payments are going to be. With an ARM, you never really know.

However, for a remodeler, I almost always recommend an ARM—not just any kind of adjustable-rate mortgage, however, but a very specific type. Note: The turning point is usually around three years. If you're going to be living in the property for longer than three years, you may be better off with a fixed rate if the interest rate is low at the time you secure it. (If the rate is high, you may want to get an ARM initially and then switch to a fixed when rates drop.)

■ DESIGNING YOUR IDEAL MORTGAGE

Perhaps the best way to talk about the right mortgage for remodel-ing is not to describe a particular loan that's out there (because there are so many and because they vary by lending institution, time and location) but instead to describe the ideal mortgage. Once we know the ideal and understand why it's so good, we can seek out one as close to it as possible.

The big reason why an ARM is an ideal mortgage is that the initial interest rate is usually low. With an ARM we typically will get a low teaser rate for the first few months or years of the mortgage. If you're planning to keep the property a relatively short time (typically under two years), this initial low rate fits in perfectly. Let's consider it more closely.

The ideal remodel mortgage would be an ARM with the following:

1. A low teaser rate

2. Short steps

3. Long adjustment periods

The Teaser

ARMs benefit the lender more than the borrower because the interest rate can move up or down depending on market conditions. Therefore, given a choice between an ARM and a fixed-rate mortgage, most borrowers would prefer the fixed rate.

For this reason, lenders have to sweeten the pot in order to get borrowers to go for ARMs. They do this with a teaser rate. This is a below-market initial rate that gets you hooked on the mortgage. Once you've gotten the loan, the rate moves up until it's at par with the market.

The important thing to remember when you're getting a mortgage for a remodel is to keep your long-term goals straight. If you're planning to live in the house indefinitely, you may want to consider a fixed-rate mortgage. On the other hand, if you're planning to resell fairly soon, you're in an ideal position to take advantage of this teaser rate, in essence taking advantage of the lenders.

Yes, you'll take their below-market teaser. If all goes well, by the time the rate moves up to par with the market, you'll sell the property and pay off the mortgage.

Be sure you understand what's being done here. Normally, the teaser is a below-market introductory rate to induce you to get an ARM. The lender hopes you'll keep that ARM for seven to ten years. The teaser lasts only a year or two at the most. The rest of the time, the mortgage is at market rates.

What you do is lock in that teaser. By the time the interest rate rises to par with market, you've finished the remodel and sold the property. Let's take an example.

Locking In a Teaser Rate

Harold was looking for the lowest possible mortgage interest rate when buying a property to remodel. The average market rate (fixed and ARM) was 10 percent at the time. However, one lender had a teaser rate of 7 percent. Because Harold was borrowing $100,000, that was a difference in payments of $878 versus $665, or a savings of $213 a month. Certainly, it made sense for Harold to consider the ARM with the low teaser rate.

> For a remodeling mortgage, you want to get as low a teaser rate as possible.

Get Short Steps

However, be forewarned. The teaser rate isn't all you need to look for. There are also the steps. What, you may reasonably ask, are the steps? ARMs all have limitations on the maximum amount that the interest rate can move up or down in any given period. These are called steps. For example, an ARM may have steps of 2 percent. This means that in each adjustment period, the interest rate can vary up or down a maximum of 2 percent.

If Harold's mortgage had 2 percent steps, that would mean that in the first adjustment period, the interest rate would go up 2 percent. Why? Because Harold's teaser rate was 7 percent and the market rate was 10 percent. The lender wants to get the mortgage paying at the market rate as soon as possible. Hence, at the next opportunity, the lender is sure to raise the rate the maximum step, in this case, 2 percent. Very shortly, Harold's interest rate is going to move from 7 percent to 9 percent and as soon as possible after that, to 10 or 11 percent (depending on how the mortgage was written—ARMs often end up half a point or more above market after the teaser is gone).

> For a remodel mortgage, it's important to get steps that are as small as possible. Try to get steps no larger than 1 percent. If possible, get 3/4 percent or 1/2 percent maximum steps.

Adjustment Periods

Finally, there's the time between adjustments. Lenders can adjust their mortgages as often as every month or as seldom as every five or ten years. It all depends on the terms written into the loan agreement. If the adjustment period is one month, for example, and the steps are 1 percent, Harold's loan would be up to market rate in just three months. Each month for three months, the lender would raise the rate 1 percent and by the end of month three, Harold would be paying the market rate of 10 percent. That's not a good result at all.

What Harold wants are long adjustment periods. For example, let's say that his adjustment period is one year and the maximum step is 1 percent. At the end of the first year, the lender can raise the rate from 7 to 8 percent. At the end of the second year, the lender can go from 8 to 9 percent. Finally, only at the end of the third year can the lender raise the rate to 10 percent, which was the market rate when Harold got the mortgage.

> For a remodel mortgage, you want the longest adjustment periods possible.

In short, the ideal mortgage for a remodeler has a low teaser rate, short steps and a long adjustment period. Ideally, the benefit of the teaser would not end until you're ready to sell. For example, if you plan to hold the property for one year, you would want a teaser rate that would last that long. Of course, the reason is that you would end up with lower than market interest rates for your entire period of ownership!

Shortcomings of ARMs

Is that all you have to watch out for? No, there are a few other items to consider. What if you can't sell? Then you are stuck with the ARM until you can sell. You could see the advantages of the teaser lost to higher-than-market interest rates later on.

Basically, here are the items to be wary of in a remodel ARM.

■ Index: You want an index that isn't going to shoot up. Most people look for an index that has stayed fairly constant over the past several decades.

■ Margin: The margin is the difference between the index and the interest rate you are charged. You want a fair margin, one that brings the interest rate up to market, not higher than market.

■ Negative amortization: Some mortgages have a cap, or maximum amount that the payment rises each adjustment period. The problem is that there is usually no cap on the interest rate. The result is that interest due but not paid on the mortgage is added to the principal. You end up owing more than you borrowed and paying interest on interest! Stay away from this type of mortgage as though it were the plague.

■ Prepayment penalty: This is a new/old wrinkle in which the lender charges for interest it would have gotten if you had kept the mortgage longer. Paying it off early, say in two years instead of ten, costs you a sometimes sizeable penalty. Avoid this condition.

■ PREARRANGED TOTAL HOME REMODELING MORTGAGES

The goal here is to arrange for both the money to purchase the home and the money to do the remodeling at the time the purchase is made.

Can this really be done? Certainly. It's done all the time. There are two ways to handle it. One way is to arrange a maximum first mortgage to purchase the property and then, at the same time, arrange for a home-improvement second mortgage to be paid as soon as you begin work remodeling. In other words, you go through all the steps noted at the beginning of this chapter.

The only difference is that you go through them before buying. Thus, you know up front that if there's going to be a problem (and if you've written the purchase contract so that it's contingent on your getting the needed financing—see your agent and/or attorney), you can back out.

The Holdback Mortgage

There is another way, and the smartest remodelers use it. It's called holdback mortgage. Not all lenders offer this type of loan, however, so you'll have to shop around to find it. Check out small banks and savings and loans in your area that specialize in construction loans. They are the most likely lenders. A holdback mortgage means that not all of the money being loaned is given to you at once. Rather, a certain portion is given and another portion is held back. The following example illustrates how it works.

A Holdback Example. Harriet wanted to buy a house to remodel. She found the property, but wasn't sure how to get the financing for both the house and for the work to be done on it.

She went to a lender that said it would make two appraisals on the property. The first would be based on its present condition. The second would be based on the work she planned to do (taken from her description and set of plans) and would be based on the future value of the property when the work was done. (See Chapter 11 to figure out this amount.)

The lender would loan her 80 percent of the value of the property when it was finished, but would fund only 80 percent of the current value when she bought the property. The balance would be held back and given to her only as she did the work.

The property was appraised at $160,000 when the work was completed. Its current value, however, was only $110,000 (which also happened to be the purchase price). Thus the lender would make an immediate loan of 80 percent of $110,000, or $88,000. This would allow Harriet to buy the property, putting 20 percent down.

Later, as Harriet completed work on the property, the lender would advance more money, up to $128,000. In terms of time, the cash flow looked like this:

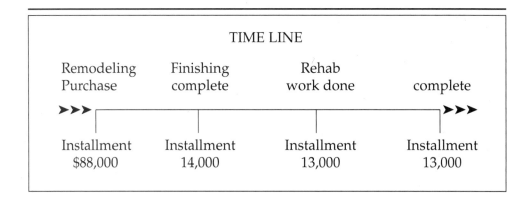

TIME LINE

Remodeling Purchase	Finishing complete	Rehab work done	complete
Installment $88,000	Installment 14,000	Installment 13,000	Installment 13,000

Establishing a time line is important for both you and the lender because it shows what work is to be done and when money is to be paid out. It avoids any confusion.

Harriet got 80 percent of the $110,000 purchase price when she bought the property and another $40,000 (in installments) as she did work on it. Her total investment was the down payment of $22,000.

In order for a holdback to work, you must have a very clear idea of what work you want to do and how much it will cost. You must be able to convince the lender that you can do it within set time constraints. A good set of plans and a workable time line are essential.

The advantage of the holdback mortgage is that it allows you to arrange for remodel financing before you make the purchase. That way, there are no surprises later. You know for sure that the money to do the remodel work is ready and available when you need it. (Also ask your lender about FHA 203K, which works in a similar way with 5 percent or less down.)

■ OTHER TYPES OF FINANCING

So far we have considered only one type of financing: You get a new loan for both purchase and remodel work. However, there are other ways to finance the deal.

Assumptions

Sometimes, depending on the area of the country, you can assume the seller's existing loan. Today only two types of loans are assumable for practical purposes. The first type are government guaranteed or insured loans such as VA and FHA mortgages. The second are ARMs, most of which are assumable only if you qualify at the current market rate.

Note that VA and FHA loans are no longer freely assumable, as they were in the past. Depending on when they were placed on the property, you may need to submit an application and credit report to assume them.

You have to ask yourself: Why would I want to assume a loan rather than get a new one? There is only one answer—it's cheaper. You must then decide if it is indeed cheaper. An old FHA or VA loan may have a much lower interest rate. This makes it a good assumption possibility. The problem is that usually an older loan is written for substantially less than the purchase price. In other words, it isn't a big enough mortgage.

If that's the case, then consider assuming an existing first mortgage and getting a new second mortgage, from either an institution or a seller, for most of the difference. We'll cover both of these shortly.

ARMs are usually assumable and may have large enough balances to be worthwhile because they are usually fairly recent loans.

However, with an ARM you get the current market rate and, as noted, you have to qualify fully. The advantage is that the cost of getting the loan, points and title insurance is usually greatly reduced. Thus, there might be some cost advantage in assuming an ARM as well.

Institutional Seconds

Don't overlook this possibility. Lenders such as banks and savings and loans are making great second mortgages. These are often for very close to the market interest rate for firsts and they are typically for 15 years or longer. Sometimes when you're remodeling it makes more sense to assume a seller's existing financing and get a new institutional second than it does to get a new first loan to cover the purchase. Additionally, once you've purchased the remodel property, you may be able to get an institutional second combined with a holdback clause so that it's based not on current value but on future value. This could then be used to finance your remodel work.

Note: Institutional second ARMs are also available. These often have low teaser rates just like a first. You may be able to save a ton of finance money by getting a second mortgage ARM for the remodel period and then paying it off early when you sell!

Seller Financing

Another very good source of financing is the seller. If the existing first is assumable, put 10 percent down and have the seller carry the balance. In a slow market with a crummy property (which is what a remodel looks like), a seller might just go along.

With seller financing you can negotiate the terms. For example, you can insist on a lower-than-market interest rate, payments of interest only or no payments with a balloon when the house is sold! Don't overlook the seller-financing angle. (You get seller financing by insisting on it in the purchase contract, if the seller is agreeable.)

■ ═ C H A P T E R   1 3 ═ ■

Understanding Taxes and Remodeling

The first question many remodelers ask with regard to taxes is, Are there any special incentives for those in the field? Do remodelers get special treatment at tax time?

The answer is no, and yes. From the average person who remodels a portion of his or her home to the total home remodelers, there are some tax advantages, but these aren't usually directed specifically at remodeling.

In this chapter we're going to consider several ways that those who remodel can get tax advantages, first for the small project and then for the total home remodel. However, it's important to understand that we are just trying to get an overview so you'll have some idea where to go next. Tax laws are like rivers—always in motion. New laws come in, and there are new interpretations of existing laws. The Internal Revenue Service frequently issues new and revised guidelines on taxation. This flux indicates that even though an effort has been made to see that the material in this chapter is accurate, no guarantee can be given on its accuracy with regard to current tax law. As a consequence, you should not rely on any material that's presented in this chapter. Further, neither the author nor the publisher is involved in giving tax advice. For up-to-date tax information and advice, contact a tax professional.

■ DEDUCTIONS FOR REMODELING A PRINCIPAL RESIDENCE

First, let's consider the tax rules when you're remodeling your principal residence. Your principal residence is the home in which you spend most of your time each year. You have to actually live there. It can't be a rental unit. It can't be a house that you work on but don't live in. You have to actually set up residency in the premises. It can, however, be a single family house, a duplex, a condo or co-op, even a mobile home or in some cases a boat!

Interest Deductions

When you do a small remodeling job on your home (principal residence), you may take out a home equity mortgage (see Chapter 12 for financing alternatives) to pay for the project. The interest you pay on this mortgage may be fully deductible, provided the entire mortgage is used for home improvement.

There are essentially two types of mortgages, as far as the IRS is concerned, when it comes to home remodeling. If the work being done is on your principal or main residence or on your vacation home, the interest on any mortgage used for improving the property is deductible up to a million dollars of combined mortgage value. (All the mortgages the taxpayer has on a principal residence and one additional vacation home cannot equal more than a million dollars at the time of this writing.) If the work being done is for any other reason, the maximum is $100,000 of mortgage value.

Adding to the Tax Base

You can also get some tax benefit from any remodeling work that improves your home (again principal residence), provided you keep accurate records. However, to understand how this works we have to spend a moment and take a step back into the somewhat arcane world of income taxation.

All property, as far as the IRS is concerned, has a basis. This is usually what you paid for it. It's the purchase price plus your costs of purchase, which include closing costs and loan costs not deductible immediately. (We'll cover those shortly.) Your basis can be increased by any improvements you make to the property, and that's what we're concerned with here.

For example, let's say you buy a home to live in for $100,000 and your costs of purchase amount to another $5,000. Your basis is now $105,000.

Let's say that you remodel the kitchen and keep accurate records, which show you spent $5,000 for materials. Now your basis has jumped up to $110,000.

Price	$100,000
Costs	5,000
Basis	105,000
Improvements	5,000
Adjusted basis	110,000

No, you can't deduct the remodeling improvements from your income. However, you can save money when it's time to sell. Let's say that you sell your property for $130,000. Now you sold for more than you paid, so you will have a taxable gain or profit. How much is it?

Let's say that it cost you $10,000 in closing costs, including commission to sell. You now deduct this from your sale price.

Sale price	130,000
Sale cost	−10,000
Adjusted sale price	120,000

To find your gain, you subtract your basis, adjusted for improvements, from your sale price, adjusted for sale costs. It looks like this:

Before Improvements		**After Improvements**	
Adjusted sale price	120,000		120,000
Basis	100,000	Adjusted basis	110,000
Taxable gain (profit)	20,000		10,000

The improvements to your property made when remodeling have acted to raise your basis and this has helped you reduce your gain when you sold.

Remember, however, that not all remodeling expenses are improvements, although most probably are. Anything that adds value to your property that is not considered repair or maintenance is probably an improvement.

■ DEFERRAL RULES

Even though there is still some tax to pay in our example above, it might be deferred (not forgiven, but rolled over into the future). If the home is your principal residence and you meet some fairly strict guidelines, you can defer the entire tax on your gain provided you purchase another principal residence of equal or greater value within a two-year period.

You've probably heard of this rule; it's fairly well-known. What is not so well-known is that there are some restrictions that apply especially to remodelers.

Dealer in Real Estate

First off, the rule is intended to help home owners to sell and then purchase another home. It is not intended to help anyone in business. Therefore, if remodeling is your full-time business, you probably don't qualify. If all you do is buy and sell rehabbed homes, you may be classified as a dealer in real estate and the rollover benefits may be denied. You may have to calculate your gain and pay taxes each time you sell.

You should check with your accountant to see specifically what you must do to avoid being labeled a dealer in real estate. Generally, you can avoid this designation if you have another full-time occupation, such as being employed by someone or running your own business in another field. Also, if there is a significant time lag between the purchase and sale of the rehabbed home, it will be hard for anyone to say that you didn't simply buy and fix up a principal residence. People who are not remodelers do this all the time.

In short, if you remodel part-time and you live in the property for several years before selling, you can probably avoid being designated as being in the remodeling business.

Time-Period Requirements

Many people are aware that they can defer all the gain on the sale of a principal residence provided that they purchase another residence of equal or greater value within two years before or after the sale.

There are other restrictions that are beyond the scope of this book and that your accountant can explain. However, there are two of them that many people may not be aware of. First, a part of the gain may be deferred even if the new home that is purchased costs less than you sold the old one for. The calculation is fairly complex and should be handled by your accountant. Just be aware that you don't have to buy another home for more than the cost of the last home to get some of the benefit from the deferral.

The second point that most people are unaware of, and that particularly affects remodelers, is that you can do this only once every two years. If you purchase home A, resell in one year, purchase home B and resell within a second year to purchase home C, you can defer the gain between homes A and C. The gain you make on the purchase and sale of home B may be construed as fully taxable in the year received.

In other words, in order to take advantage of the deferral on sale of a principal residence, you really must be a part-time rehabber who lives in the property you are working on. Of course, this is the classical way to remodel. You buy a home, move in and fix it up while you're living there, and then eventually sell. Along the way you can take out your profits (they don't have to be reinvested in the new home) and continually move up to bigger and better homes.

Finally, you might be wondering, how long can you keep it up? The answer is until you retire or die! When you reach age 55, you may be entitled to a once-in-a-lifetime exclusion of up to $125,000 of your gain!

■ DEDUCTIONS FOR A HOME REMODELING BUSINESS

As noted, thus far we're talking only about tax advantages for part-time remodelers working on their own residences. What if you buy a fixer-upper, don't live in it while doing renovations, and then sell for profit? In other words, you're doing it as a business. Are there any deductions for you?

If you're operating a home remodeling business, you should be able to deduct your normal business expenses in the year that they occur. This includes an office, phone and mailings. If you have a car or truck, it may also be deductible, along with depreciation on the vehicles and repairs and maintenance. You may also be able to deduct your gasoline cost or take a standard mileage charge.

Be aware that you'll have to document everything. You'll have to account for every mile driven for a business purpose as opposed to a pleasure purpose. There are strict limitations. For example, you may have to demonstrate that more than half of the use of the vehicle was for business. The cost of the vehicle will also be limited.

Moreover, there will be many seemingly obvious deductions that you cannot take. For example, the drive from your home to your office (which may be the remodeling site) is probably not deductible. You normally can't deduct the costs of getting to work. However, if you leave the office and travel 30 miles each way to a lumberyard to pick up some supplies, the cost of that trip may be fully deductible!

When It's an Investment

On the other hand, let's say that you're not operating a home remodeling business, but instead have another full-time job. You're doing remodeling part time. You've found a fixer-upper and are renovating it. The property is an investment, much like a rental. What deductions can you take?

If the property is an investment held for income production (rental), you can take your expenses that are not capital improvements, subject to the active/passive rules described shortly.

Capital Improvement versus Expense

A large part of what you can deduct depends on whether the work done was a capital improvement or an operating expense. A capital improvement must be added to the basis, as explained earlier. An operating expense is something that usually involves repair or maintenance. It can be used to offset income from the property (if any) during the year and if there's a loss, that might be written off against your ordinary income (from your regular job), subject to the active/passive real estate rules.

The test for the difference between a capital improvement and a maintenance expense is often tricky. For example, the home may have a central heater that doesn't work. You put in a new heater, simply replacing the old. Is that maintenance or improvement? My guess is that the government would call that a capital improvement and might require you to capitalize the expense over the life of the heater. On the other hand, let's say the existing heater needed a new thermostat that cost $100. My guess is that this might be considered an allowable and deductible expense. (My own experience is that if the item costs under a couple hundred dollars and it replaces an existing item, it usually can be expensed in the year purchased. On the other hand, if it's a new item or costs more than a couple hundred dollars, it generally must be capitalized over its allowable life.)

If the item is a capital improvement, it must be depreciated over its life span. This now gets into the rather difficult subject of depreciation rules. Check with your accountant about how to handle depreciation of items on your property.

The Active/Passive Real Estate Rules

Before 1986, virtually all investments were treated in the same way for tax purposes. The 1986 act, however, created separate categories of investments for tax purposes. These included the following:

- Active activities, such as regular work or a business you operated

- Portfolio activities, such as bonds or interest-bearing accounts that you owned

- Passive activities, in which you did not participate in the business

All real estate was automatically classified as a passive activity. This had some unfortunate consequences, the most important of which was that losses from real estate (passive) could not be used to offset gains in another area (active or portfolio). In other words, any losses you sustained while operating a real estate activity, such as a rental house, could not be deducted from your regular income derived from your work.

This was a major blow to real estate investors. For example, let's say that you owned a rental house. Your rental income was $1,000 per month. Figuring a month's vacancy for re-renting, the house brought in $11,000 per year.

Your expenses, including mortgage, taxes, interest and insurance, came to $1,100 per month, or $13,200 per year. Add to this some of the allowance costs you had for remodeling and for depreciation, and the total could easily be well over $20,000. In other words, you lost a considerable amount of money operating the property.

However, because it was a passive investment, you could not deduct the loss from your regular (active) income! The loss was carried forward and was deducted from any gain when you eventually sold the property. Let's take an example.

Passive Activity Losses

Rental-house income (annual)		$11,000
Rental-house expenses		
Mortgage, taxes, insurance (annual)	$13,200	
Depreciation	4,000	
Rehab costs taken	5,000	
Total expenses	22,200	−22,200
First year loss		−11,200

In the first year of ownership of this hypothetical home, you lost $11,200, of which all but $4,000 (depreciation) was an actual cash out-of-pocket expense. Yet because real estate is defined as a passive investment, you can't take a deduction that year against your regular income!

The Exclusion

Those in Congress who drafted the new tax laws realized the enormous burden this would place on small investors, so they provided an exclusion. The exclusion works like this:

> You can deduct up to $25,000 of passive real estate losses from your active income, provided your gross income is under $100,000. For every dollar your income exceeds $100,000 you lose $0.50 of the exclusion. By the time you reach $150,000 the entire exclusion is lost.

There are a few other strict restrictions, which include the fact that you must actively be involved in the management of the rental real estate. You have to make the decisions regarding tenants and expenditures (even if you hire a management firm to handle the property for you). What this all means is that as long as you don't earn too much money, you can still get many of the deductions that were available before 1986.

■ SELLING AND CAPITAL GAINS

A large amount of your gain when you sell your investment remodeling home may have to be paid in taxes. However, if you have been adding the various improvements to your tax base (see our earlier example), the bite should be far less deep.

Remember, you can add the costs of purchase as well as the costs of improvements to your tax base. This probably includes most of your remodeling expenses.

A Tax on Sale Example. Sandra recently sold her remodel home in the same year she bought it. The deductions she took and the taxes she paid may be helpful in illustrating what is and is not usually done.

Purchase price	$105,000
Plus costs of purchase	+ 5,000
Adjusted purchase price	= 110,000

Costs of rehabbing	
Materials	+ 11,000
Hired labor	+ 3,000
Business expenses	+ 3,000
Interest on mortgage	+ 6,000
Total rehab costs	+ 23,000
Adjusted tax base	= 133,000
Sale price	$ 215,000
Less costs of sale	−15,000
	= 200,000
Capital gain	67,000
Tax calculation (federal and state tax brackets) ×	39%
Tax owed	26,130
Net gain after taxes, including personal labor spent	40,870

Note: The calculations shown above are for purposes of illustrating this example only. The IRS requires a different format when showing capital gains.

Sandra earned $67,000 on the remodel project, including what she considered her profit and her labor. However, she ended up paying roughly 28 percent of the gain to the federal government and another 11 percent to the state.

Needless to say, she was angry at having to pay so much in taxes. As far as she was concerned, a lot of her profits and perhaps even some of her labor were eaten up in taxes. To her it seemed as though she had taken an enormous risk and spent a lot of time and effort working on the project, only to find that the government was taking all the gravy. Of course, if it had been her principal residence, instead of an investment, she could have rolled over the entire gain into another property and deferred all of her taxes to the future. (Note: By the time you read this, a reduction in the capital gains tax by Congress may soften the blow considerably.)

■ THE TAX PROBLEM

What we've seen in this chapter is that tax law today is a real can of worms. For the average person, just understanding how to deal with it can be overwhelming.

On the other hand, not knowing the tax consequences of any actions you take can be disastrous. For example, if you remodel a home and then rent it out, only to discover later that you can't deduct many of your remodel expenses in the year they were done, you could have a big problem.

The best advice is to see a good accountant early on. Learn what the tax problems peculiar to your deal are and how to handle them. In this way you can avoid feeling your heart palpitate and your stomach sink on April 15.

Additionally, to repeat a piece of advice I follow myself, in today's tax climate, try to live in the house you remodel so you can claim it as your principal residence (following the appropriate rules). This can save you many tax dollars.

For details on special tax incentives for historical renovation, check with your accountant.

Rehabbing Commercial Property

Normally, most remodelers who like big projects stick exclusively to homes. However, there are still opportunities in commercial remodeling (rehabbing), probably far more than in homes, because of the real estate recession of the late 1980s and early 1990s.

All real estate was forced down during this period. However, the hardest hit was commercial real estate, including office space and stores. Literally tens of thousands of these properties were put into foreclosure. Even the government, through the Resolution Trust Corporation (RTC), was faced with disposing of a great deal of this kind of property.

Although commercial property is rebounding in some areas, there are still many fixer-uppers available. For the enterprising individual, this field can still be a gold mine.

■ THE PROBLEM OF FIXER-UPPER COMMERCIAL PROPERTY

The problem with much of the foreclosed commercial property available today is that it is run-down. Usually it's not too old, rarely over ten years. But the original owner is long gone, and the succeeding owners, first the developer, then the bank and eventually, perhaps, the government, have allowed the properties to deteriorate. Many are in terrible shape.

All of which promises a real opportunity to a creative and ambitious rehabber. Why not buy one (or more) of these commercial properties and rehab it? Can the rewards justify the risks?

I think the rewards can more than justify the risks in many cases. Here's why.

Reward versus Risk with Commercial Rehabbing

The big risk in commercial rehabbing is that you aren't likely to be able to sell for much of a profit in the immediate future. There's simply too much similar property on the market to allow prices to rise.

As a result, you're going to have to hang onto it for a while after you finish rehabbing. You'll have to be able to rent the property for your expenses and hang on for as long as five years, until the normal expansion of the country catches up with the supply. At that time, the rewards kick in.

The reason for the potential rewards is simple. It's not likely that much new commercial real estate is going to be built during the next few years. Even if developers and builders want to put it up, few banks are going to stick their necks out by giving construction loans at a time when so much commercial real estate is in foreclosure.

To recap, the risk is that you can't sell immediately, and unless you're careful, and perhaps even a bit lucky, you'll have a tough time renting for your expenses. In short, you could lose the property.

The reward is that if you hang onto it, you could make a fortune once the market turns around.

■ WHAT'S INVOLVED IN COMMERCIAL REAL ESTATE REHABBING?

If this brief overview has you interested, let's delve a bit further into the field. What's actually involved in commercial real estate rehabbing?

You'll recall that in an earlier chapter we discussed location. I noted that homebuyers tend to purchase neighborhoods before houses.

Location, I emphasized, was the most important factor in value. When it comes to commercial real estate, location becomes almost the only factor. It doesn't matter whether it's a small strip shopping center, a large mall-type center or an office space—what will most determine success or failure is location.

What's interesting about the current commercial real estate market is that many properties with reasonably good locations are still available at low prices. (Most of the really terrific locations are still quoting high prices.)

Consequently, if you're interested in rehabbing commercial real estate, the first thing you need to do is to find run-down properties in great locations. (If that sounds like rehabbing homes, you're not far off.)

Sources

Your source for information on suitable commercial real estate includes agents. In larger offices there are typically one or two agents who specialize in commercial properties. (Everyone else sells houses.) You need to contact these special agents.

To avoid bringing too many agents into the picture (each of whom will want a piece of the commission, thus making the right agents less willing to work with you), I recommend simply calling a real estate office and asking to talk to the agent who handles commercial real estate or office space. Sometimes offices handle leasing, and if you call the leasing agent, he or she can direct you to the agent who handles commercial sales, or perhaps even to the owners themselves.

Of course, not all commercial real estate is listed with agents. Some properties are still owned by the Resolution Trust Corporation (as of this writing). It will provide you with locations, appraisals and everything else you need to examine and evaluate its properties. A broker can provide you with the RTC's current phone number.

Finally, there are FSBOs. Unlike homes, a great amount of commercial and office real estate is sold directly by owners when the market is bad. Look for ads in the local newspapers. Drive by properties. Often, the only notice that a property is for sale will be a sign, not always a large sign, on the property itself.

Evaluation

Evaluating a commercial property is somewhat different from evaluating a house. The big difference, and what to be alert for, are the selling points. With a home, you're attuned to kitchens and baths. With commercial properties, though it's good to have nice-looking bathrooms, they aren't usually going to appeal to a buyer or a tenant.

Location. Rather, what you're usually looking for is exposure. We've already touched on this in terms of location. If it's purely commercial, you need a good location on a heavily trafficked street. If it's office space, a good commercial location doesn't hurt. But being isolated on a side street, a killer for purely commercial, isn't always so bad for offices if there is ample parking.

The ideal commercial rehab is one that is on a heavily trafficked street, and the building is about ten years old and completely dilapidated. You get the benefit of the location and the lower price that comes from not only a bad market, but a run-down property.

Neighborhood. Just as with homes, the neighborhood influence is also important. This is particularly true of smaller buildings. With a large building or mall, the commercial property, in essence, creates its own neighborhood environment. For a mall owner, the biggest concern often is proximity to freeway offramps.

With small strip shops or office buildings, you want to be near other similar businesses so that the combined effect is to bring in more customers. Of course, there's also a downside. Today, many older commercial and office buildings are in deteriorating neighborhoods with crime problems. The personal safety aspect could drive customers and tenants away. I never buy anything in a neighborhood where I'm afraid to walk in the evening.

Access. It's also important to have easy access. You could have a building on a heavily trafficked street, but if it's impossible to turn off the street into your parking lot or to pull out from your parking lot into the street, you've got a real problem and a detracting feature that you can't correct. Bad access means fewer customers.

Although it is possible to live without access from both directions of traffic on the street (a left turn into or out of the property may be difficult or impossible), you'd better be darn sure you have at least one direction of good access.

Parking. Yet another consideration is ample parking. This is often the biggest hang-up with older small units. The original builder/developer may have underestimated how many parking spaces would be needed and the zoning and building department may have gone along. As a result, you may have only two or three spaces per rental unit when you actually need five or six.

Not having adequate parking can mean that customers have a tough time getting in and out and decide to go elsewhere in the future. As a result you lose, or have difficulty in getting, tenants.

Presentation. Finally there's the matter of how the property looks to someone approaching it. This is where your rehabbing skills come into play. What you want, ideally, is a property with the following characteristics:

- Great location

- Good neighborhood

- Easy access

- Adequate parking

- Terrible presentation

A bad presentation or appearance is bad for the property, good for the rehabber. A bad presentation can take a variety of forms. It can be as simple as the building needing paint and the windows needing to be cleaned. Or it can involve having an ugly entrance or ugly appearance from the street, necessitating a rehab of the entire front.

If you can find a building that has all the other desirable attributes (location, neighborhood, access and parking) and lacks only a good presentation, you may have your rehab treasure. In a bad real estate market, such as we've been experiencing lately, an awful presentation by itself can be enough to cause a loss of business and of tenants and a foreclosure.

Although you can't easily correct problems with location, neighborhood, access or parking, you can correct problems with presentation. You can rip off the current front of the building and replace it with a new facade and entrance. You can repave the parking lot and the entrance drive. You can pour concrete or lay bricks for a new walkway. You can plant attractive shrubs.

This is not to say that any of the rehab improvements you make won't be expensive—they may be. The improvements will count a lot when there isn't some other big and noncorrectable detracting feature (such as a bad neighborhood or poor access).

Interior. Often the interior of an office building or commercial location is the easiest to handle. With commercial property, the tenant may want to take care of the interior itself. Depending on the leasing structure, you may create an interior treatment based on the tenant's specifications.

For office space, typically all that's required is a high-quality grade of carpet that looks good and lasts and plain walls painted white. Adequate heating and cooling are also requirements, and occasionally cleaning the outside of the windows doesn't hurt.

In short, most of the real tough rehabbing work you'll need to do will very likely be in the presentation of the property. There's usually relatively little that you need to worry about with regard to the inside.

Costs

It's difficult to compare costs between residential remodeling and commercial rehabbing. With a house, there are a lot of easy-to-do items that are obvious—you know that you need to come up with a good-looking kitchen and bath.

With a commercial property, often the hardest part is getting the right concept. Finding out what to do that will look good for the smallest amount of money can be the really big task. I always recommend a commercial architect. This is an architect who has had specific experience in small commercial centers or office space. He or she should be able to give you some ideas and create some plans to fit your specific needs.

Until you have your plans and estimates of cost, however, you won't know exactly how much to spend. Keep in mind that it's going to be expensive. See Chapter 3 for information on calculating costs, but also try to work with an architect or builder before you buy so that you have some idea of what you're tackling. Fortunately, with commercial and office property these days, there aren't too many people lining up to buy, so you should have plenty of time to get accurate estimates before you commit yourself.

Vacancies

Finally, before you buy, get a good handle on vacancy rates. In some cities the office-space vacancy rate is nearly 40 percent! Just to get office space rented, owners may give away several months rent-free or knock the square-footage costs down significantly. You'll be competing in that market. If the vacancy rate is high, make sure that you've bought at a low enough price to at least break even and hold onto your property until better days.

Giving It a Try

If you want a real challenge, consider rehabbing office or commercial space. In this chapter we've had just a taste of what's involved. Keep in mind that even though it's also called remodeling, it's really a different ball game. Only part of what you learn in remodeling a home will apply to commercial and office property.

Be prepared to make mistakes and to give yourself enough margin to cover them. Just remember, if you do succeed, the profits can be gigantic!

■ = CHAPTER 15 = ■

Avoiding Remodeling Pitfalls

As in any other endeavor, there are always pitfalls. These are the hidden disasters you can blunder into, turning an otherwise fun and profitable venture into one that causes real headaches and possibly even loses vast amounts of money. As any remodeler who has had a project go bad can tell you, there's nothing much worse than to put your sweat and hope into remodeling only to find out that the job looks terrible or that when it comes time to sell, you lose money.

Although it is impossible to anticipate all the problems you could run into as a remodeler, in this chapter I am listing the six that I think are the biggest and worst pitfalls. If there's nothing else you take away from this book, I hope it will be the insights you get here.

■ YOU TRY TO DO TOO MUCH YOURSELF

Let's face it, the way most of us remodel is to cut costs to the bare bones. Every dollar we don't spend renovating the property is another dollar in our pocket. The simplest way of cutting costs is to do the work ourselves.

What I'm getting at is reiterating a point made back in Chapter 5. The point is that sometimes we can take on too much ourselves. It's one thing to try to save money; it's another to end up with inferior quality, delays or incomplete jobs. In other words, it's important not to be penny wise and pound foolish.

The great problem here is that it's often a thin dividing line between whether it's best to do the job ourselves or to have someone else do it. Here's an example.

I recently wanted to renovate a bathroom. The tiles around the tub were cracked and falling out. They were not salvageable. In addition, the tub itself had some fairly deep pits and rust stains.

I was faced with several decisions. Should I have the tub resurfaced, which would cost about $250, but had to be handled by a professional? Should I instead get a new tub? Should I replace the tiles with new ones or should I instead put in a fiberglass enclosure? What about the walls around the tub, which showed evidence of rot and other water damage? Should I have the walls ripped out and replaced? Or should I simply try to patch? And what about the faucets, which were old and paint-coated?

My goal was a modernized bathroom that would eventually help sell the home, so I decided to remodel it all. However, the house was moderately priced, so I didn't think it justified installing new tiles. I would have the tub renovated, put in new faucets, pull out the old tile and put in new wallboard and a new fiberglass stall. It should come out looking like new.

The next question was, should I do it myself or have someone else do it? The problem was that I was under a tight work schedule with other projects I had. I wanted to get this bathroom done right away so it could be used.

I figured that the materials would cost about $600 (tub refinishing, new fiberglass stalls, wallboard and faucets). However, the job was labor-intensive. I figured it would take me the better part of a week to get in there and do it all just right. On the other hand, I could hire a pro to come and do it for about $400 in labor.

What should I do? Should I do the work myself? It certainly was within my capabilities. Or should I hire a pro to do it and pay an extra $400?

I'm quite sure that some readers are snickering to themselves, thinking, "Do it yourself. After all, you're a remodeler, aren't you?"

Others may be thinking, "Hire it out. You have other work that you can be doing."

Here, as in most decisions we have to make, the answer is not clear-cut. I didn't want to spend the extra $400 in labor. On the other hand, I wanted to get the job done quickly.

With some misgivings, I had someone else do the work. The results proved enlightening. It turned out that the tub, which I would have refinished, was not salvageable. It was too far gone and had to be replaced. To get it out meant breaking into the wall on one side of the bathroom and buying and installing a new tub.

However, the pro I had doing the work managed to find a brand new tub at a local discount house for just $80 (remember the Rule of the Single Project)! That compared with the $250 I would have had to pay for resurfacing. As a result, putting in a new tub actually saved me money! I also saved time: The pro had to fight the old tub for nearly a day to get it out. And then he had almost as much trouble getting the new one in. Along the way the old drain crumbled from age and he had to spend another day trying to find a replacement.

There were other unexpected problems. The wall rot was more extensive than I had anticipated. There were additional costs for ripping out the old wall, putting in new wallboard and taping, texturing and repainting.

The bottom line was that the job turned out to be much bigger than I had foreseen. It took the pro nearly two weeks to get it done. Had I taken it on myself, it would have put me seriously behind schedule.

On the other hand, the pro managed to find bargains here and there (such as the inexpensive tub) that cut down on the costs. I had anticipated that materials and labor would run about $1,000. It turned out the final job only cost $950. Further, had I done it myself and not been able to find the bargains that the pro found, it would have cost me close to that for materials alone!

The moral is that sometimes it is cheaper and faster to have someone else do the work.

I am sure some die-hard home remodelers are saying that this example was an exception. You can't always have someone else do the work and come out ahead. Most of the time the only way to save money is to do it yourself. My point, however, is that you should stand back and consider: Is this one of those times when it's better to hire out the work?

■ YOU DON'T REALLY LIKE REMODELING

Although there isn't a whole lot of glamour associated with remodeling, there is a certain mystique involved. Many people, particularly young couples with little or no previous experience in the building trades, see it as a kind of romantic adventure. In the extreme, they'll buy a run-down home, work together and build it into something beautiful, then sell at a large profit. Everyone will compliment them on their cleverness, and the whole episode will draw them even closer together.

In truth, this does happen. It happened to my wife and me. But it's not for everyone. Remodeling, big or small, is far from romantic. It usually starts off with cleaning up someone else's filth. Along the way you work with old, sometimes decaying pieces of wood, flooring, tiles and other materials.

There are long hours and occasionally backbreaking work. Mostly there's work with your hands. You're constantly pulling apart or putting together. You're hammering or screwing together a fixture or painting or hauling. At the end of the day your hands are likely to be rough, bruised and covered with grime. Calluses form and over time your hands take on a toughened, hardy look.

Many people just don't like this. They may like the idea of working on a project once in a while and the satisfaction of seeing it get done, but they don't like the hard work. They don't like spending hour after hour on something tedious.

In short, they like the glamour, such as it is, of remodeling. Once involved in the field, however, they quickly discover that it can be horrible. It's something they would much prefer to hire someone else to do. It's menial. It's slave labor. They just don't like it.

Where do you fit in? Will you discover that you really don't like remodeling only after tearing out a wall or, perish the thought, buying a fixer-upper?

In Chapter 2 there is a quiz you can take to help you get a better understanding of your own preferences with regard to remodeling. Many people either skip it entirely or just run through quickly. My suggestion is that you spend some time on the quiz. It might help you avoid some really big problems from getting into something that you really don't like.

■ YOU FAILED TO ACCURATELY ASSESS THE WORK NEEDED

Much of the time, most remodelers fly by the seat of their pants. After all, remodeling is the sort of thing that's done by people who love to figure out ways to rejuvenate things, who enjoy working with their hands and who don't mind taking on a challenge.

The trouble is that sometimes we begin to believe in our own infallibility. Sometimes we think that because we said or thought it, it must be true. Sometimes we forget to check things out. When this happens, we're asking for disaster. There are two big areas related to these problems where remodelers tend to fall down. The first is thoroughly checking out the job before starting. We want to remodel a closet and put in a tub, but don't go under the house to determine whether it's even possible to get sewer lines to the areas. The second is in getting expert advice. We want add a room, but don't check with a contractor to see what's likely to be involved with breaking into the existing structure.

Let's consider these problems in more detail in the case of a full home remodel. First, consider the problem of not checking things out.

After weeks of searching, you at last locate a good remodel house. The price, remarkably, is right. You can buy, remodel and sell for your wages and a profit. It's a green light, a good deal. But is it really? Did you check out the property thoroughly? Do you know the real reason the owner has lowered the price or are you looking only at the apparent reason?

The other area in which remodelers tend to be too self-assured is in their ability to judge repair work. I had a friend who bought a house in an exclusive area for about half its cost. Of course, it had a problem: it was sinking due to wet soil. He planned to sink some piles, jack the house up and then resell it.

It was a good plan, but it had a problem. He was not an engineer, and he had no knowledge of soils or structural design. Whereas sinking a pier was a good idea, it turned out that he would have had to sink that pier halfway to China before it struck solid ground. The house was built on an old marsh that went down more than 75 feet. Sinking piers that deep was prohibitively expensive.

In short, there was no cure for the house. It would continue to slip until it fell over. Shortly after he bought it, the city condemned it. His was a total loss because he couldn't even resell the lot.

I urge those of you who are doers to hold yourself back just a bit. Yes, you may very well want to get on with it, but until you've checked out the *n*th detail, you really don't know what you are dealing with. The property may seem like a gem, but it may turn out to be nothing but cheap glass.

Moreover, as much as you may think you know, you don't know everything. In some very specialized areas, in fact, you may know nothing. Just because you spent ten years as a plumber, for example, doesn't mean you know beans about soil or structural engineering.

The smartest remodelers are those who are aware of what they don't know.

Investigate all you can by yourself and then spend the usually very few bucks necessary to get expert advice. If it's only remodeling a kitchen, get a contractor in to give you a bid. You may find that there are all sorts of things that need to be done that you never even considered.

Remember, ignorance is bliss—but it's also costly.

■ YOU PAID TOO MUCH

It's probably the *biggest* blunder a full house remodeler can make. It's an easy mistake to fall into.

The problem is that there aren't many good remodel properties out there. You have to spend a lot of time hunting to find the right property and if there are a lot of remodelers active in your area, the competition can be strong.

This isn't to say that there are no good remodel properties available or that they are impossible to find. I'm only commenting on the normal human tendency to change our expectations when we can't find what we want.

Total home remodeling is business. If you pay more than you should, your business will suffer. You'll be working for less, making less, and if you do it too much or too often, you'll go out of business.

When you can't find what meets your specifications in remodeling, you can't afford to raise your price. In Chapters 10 and 11 I described how to evaluate a property by working back from the eventual resale price. We deduct our anticipated profit and the costs of the remodel work. That's the maximum price we can pay.

But what if it's the fifth house you've looked at and the seller just won't budge at that price? Let's say the anticipated resale is $100,000 after sales costs. You want $5,000 profit and your costs will be $30,000 (including an hourly minimum for your labor). You need to buy the property for $65,000. But the seller won't budge for less than $75,000. What do you do?

The mistake is to go back, sharpen your pencil and do some additional calculating. For example, you begin to think that maybe the market might improve by the time you sell and you'll be able to get $103,000 for the house. Or maybe you can sell "by owner" and save the commission. If that's the case, maybe your net will be $107,000.

On the other hand, do you really need to make a 5 percent profit? After all, you're getting paid for your time. What about whittling that profit down to 2 percent? If that's the case, then you maybe can afford to pay $75,000.

Do you see what's happening?

The deal doesn't really fit the parameters you've set out, so you're changing the parameters to fit the deal. If the seller won't go low enough to make the remodel work, you'll change the remodel to suit the seller's price.

If you've done your homework, you know exactlywhat it'll cost— $30,000. You also know that in order to make it worthwhile for you to do remodel work, you need to make (in this case) 5 percent. Furthermore, unless the market's too hot to touch, you will need an agent to resell.

By changing the parameters, you can rationalize yourself into believing that you can afford to pay as much as $75,000 for the house. But if you've done your homework, you can't afford to change your parameters. If your math shows that you can only afford to spend $65,000 for the house, then that's your top offer. Go higher than that and you've made a mistake. Go higher than that and, unless you're extremely lucky, you'll lose money. Go higher than that and you'll put yourself out of the remodel business fast!

You may find yourself arguing, "What am I supposed to do? Let the house go? For crying out loud, the seller is willing to take $25,000 below market. I would have to be a fool to let it slip by. If I don't grab it now, someone else will."

My advice is to let it go. It doesn't make any difference how much below market a house's price apparently is. What counts is your math. In the above example, the house wasn't $25,000 below market at a price of $75,000; it was $10,000 too high and the seller just wouldn't admit it!

Think of it this way: Would you be willing to pay $10,000 over what a house is worth? Would you be willing to buy an overpriced house? Go into a corner and say to yourself three times: "Pass! Pass! Pass!"

I remember one time I was bidding on a house at an auction sale. In this case the house had partially burned down. It was a major remodel job. However, the sale had attracted considerable attention. I had calculated that I could afford to pay a maximum of $52,000. The bidding very quickly reached $52,000, and then someone bid $53,500. I disregarded my own advice and bid $55,000.

Fortunately, there were bigger fools than me, and someone else bid it up to $56,000, when I took myself out of the contest. Eventually it sold for more than $60,000.

Maybe it was the competition of an auction. Maybe I was just in need of a good remodel house at the time. In any event, after the sale I really felt bad that I had lost out on the property. I felt bad until about a year later, when I met the woman who had bought it. She was recounting a tale of woe about how she had lost over $10,000 in her attempt to remodel it. Then I felt better—not over her loss, but over my good fortune at not having paid too much for the property.

My feeling is that it's better to let ten overpriced houses pass by than to buy one house and find out when I go to sell that I paid too much.

The truth is that no matter what area of the country you're in (and I come from California where prices tend to be high), there are good remodel deals available. You can't afford to waste time on the bad ones. Get out there and find just the right remodel property!

■ YOU REMODEL AS THOUGH YOU'RE GOING TO LIVE THERE FOREVER

This is a mistake that is most often made by couples who work together fixing up a house. Often, they do live there. However, the point is that the remodel project is not going to be their home forever. Rather, it's temporary. Maybe they'll want to sell for a (hoped for) profit right away. Or maybe they'll decide to have a family and want a bigger home. Or a career change may take them elsewhere. The point is, eventually we all move on. And then the costs we put into that remodeling job may come back to haunt us.

Overimproving Is the Danger

Consider a typical couple in this situation. While living in their house, they begin fixing it up as though it were their forever home. Where simple blinds would do on the window, they spend a fortune on drapes and valances. Where a medium-priced carpet would be adequate, they buy the very finest quality at the highest prices.

The problem is that they are fixing up the house for themselves, not the next owner. For themselves, they are more than willing to spend all the money they want and can afford. For the next owner, however, they should be on a budget. They should evaluate the quality of materials the house warrants and then spend that much, no more.

The real difficulty is that you can fall into this pattern and not realize it. You can begin spending on higher-quality items without even realizing what you're doing. For example, it's time to buy a new sink for the kitchen you're remodeling. A perfectly acceptable white porcelain one is available for $80. You could get a more highly polished, colored one for $140—it's only $60 difference, you argue with yourself—and eventually you get the more expensive model.

If it were only the sink, there would be no problem. But multiply the money spent on the sink by dozens and dozens of other purchases that are similarly upgraded. It doesn't take very long before the thousands of dollars add up and soon you've got an overimproved white elephant (see Chapter 4).

Develop a Style

This does not mean, however, that remodeling should cramp your style. People who have been remodeling for a while develop a style. If they're into total home remodeling, they buy only certain kinds of houses with certain kinds of problems. They become specialists, for example, in two-story homes with bad roofs and basements. Or they buy only homes that have foundation problems. Over time they learn a particular specialty, become better at it than just about anyone else and stick with it.

Along the way some remodelers have certain materials that they always use in a house. One remodeler may automatically rip out all existing handrails and replace them with polished oak. Another will always put a new pink sink in the bathroom and a beige one in the kitchen. Other remodelers stick with certain types of tile.

Some remodelers have an almost religious affinity for these touches. They begin to believe that the house won't ever resell unless they add their own special touch to it.

There's nothing wrong with developing your own style or with putting specialty items that you prefer into a remodel house. In fact, you can put in anything you want, from solid-gold doorknobs to double-story arched ceilings. However, no matter what you put in, you must first budget it.

You must determine how much improvement the house can stand. If the house warrants the expensive items and there's room in the budget for them, by all means install them. You may be right in judging that the house won't be overimproved with the purple toilet in the master bath. Just remember, for most projects the best quality may be too much. You might never be able to get your money out.

Never confuse your personal desires with the needs of the house. Every house that needs remodeling requires a certain level of quality. But beyond that level, you're simply wasting money. Unless it is going to be your own personal home, you simply can't afford to do it on a remodel.

One last point needs to be made here and that's with regard to the neighborhood. Sometimes the house itself is quite elegant. You can see yourself spending money on lots of high-quality extras. Perhaps it's a Victorian home that's nearly 100 years old. You could put thousands into restoring paneling and stairs. Finding rounded cut windows to replace broken ones could be very costly. All of that may be necessary to restore the elegant old home to its former beauty.

But it may turn out that the other houses in the neighborhood have only had minimal, pragmatic restorations. Instead of being elaborately restored, they have been modernized. The old elegant charm has been replaced with efficient plumbing and heating, with insulated walls and ceilings, with enlarged rooms and redesigned fronts. In short, the remodelers who did other houses on the street didn't share your love of the old and of renovation.

You have two choices here. The first is to go it alone. You can spend the extra bucks and renovate and restore. Or you can do what they did. Simply modernize and fix things cosmetically, probably at a fraction of the cost.

My advice is not to swim against the tide. If the other homes in the neighborhood have been remodeled a particular way, you could very well be creating a white elephant by doing yours differently. Yes, buyers would look with pleasure at what you'd done. But would they fork over the extra cash that would be necessary to justify the work?

Remember, almost all buyers purchase neighborhoods before they purchase houses. It is a thousand times harder to sell a great house in a terrible neighborhood than it is to sell a terrible house in a great neighborhood. When in Rome, do as the Romans. Don't upgrade based only on your personal tastes and don't upgrade beyond the neighborhood's threshold.

■ YOU FAILED TO GET ADEQUATE FINANCING

Because there's an entire chapter devoted to financing, you might reasonably wonder why I'm bringing it up again. The reason has to do with a very specific kind of financing, namely, raising the money to complete the remodel work. This is an area we only touched on in the earlier chapter, and it bears emphasizing here.

Unless you're very wealthy (in which case you probably won't be a remodeler), you won't be able to buy and totally remodel a house without financing. That means that you'll need to borrow not only the money to purchase the property, but also part or all of the money to pay for materials, labor (including your time) and other expenses while remodeling. In short, you'll need a continuous stream of money to complete the job.

Although I'm confident that most of my readers are fairly capable when it comes to the physical work involved in remodeling (most people don't really consider doing it unless they've had some previous success along these lines), I worry when it comes to financing. Too often financing is the last consideration, when in truth it should be the first.

I'm reminded of some advice I received years ago with regard to playing chess. You may or may not be familiar with chess, but you really don't need a deep understanding of the game to appreciate the point. Admittedly I'm not a very good chess player, but I do strive to improve my game. One of the problems I seem to have is efficiently moving my pieces around the chess board. They always seem to end up either out of play or blocking each other.

One day, a person who is a very good chess player said, "Move your bishops out of the back row immediately." In chess the more powerful pieces (the king, queen, castles and horses) are in the back row. There are also two bishops who move diagonally across the board. They are somewhat difficult to move forward, however, because you first have to get some pawns out of the way.

He went on to comment, "You'll always have something else that seems better to do at the time. Moving the bishops will always seem to be wasting a move. But in the long run, getting them out quickly will enormously improve your game."

He was right. I always did have some other move that seemed more important at the time. But forcing myself to get those bishops out did improve my game.

The same thing holds true with remodel financing. There will always be something else you'll feel that you should be working on. It could be negotiating with the seller or getting bids on work and materials or getting started hammering and renovating. But if you stop all of those other things that seem so important and spend the time needed to get adequate financing, you'll have much more success in remodeling.

There's yet another point here: getting *enough* financing. Although remodelers certainly will make efforts to get sufficient financing to purchase the house, they often fall down when it comes to getting the financing necessary to complete the remodel work. Does any of the following sound familiar?

- I'll worry about paying for the remodel work when I get to it!

- I'll get a loan.

- I've got credit.

- It won't be that hard!

- If worse comes to worst I'll pay for it with my credit cards.

- I'll borrow any money I need from my brother-in-law. When he sees what a good deal this is, he'll be thrilled to lend me the money!

What all of these statements have in common is that they put off arranging for the financing of the remodel work until after the work is started or, in the case of a total home remodel, after the property is purchased. Of course, then it's too late. Like moving the bishop out in the game of chess, there always seems to be something better to do.

Let's talk about some of the problems caused by waiting to arrange financing for remodel work. First, there's the matter of a collateralized loan from the bank. This is in the form of a home equity loan, second mortgage or other similar loan for which the property is given as security. The advantage of this type of financing is that it usually gives you the lowest interest rate.

The Trouble with Waiting To Get Financing

As noted earlier, once you begin work, you usually can't get a mortgage. You can get it only before you do any work or have any materials delivered.

Then, you never know how big a mortgage you can get until you apply. Until then, it's all speculation. So to be sure of getting as much as you need, you must apply at the time you buy the property.

As a result of not getting a mortgage before you start work, you may have to get an uncollateralized loan. Let's say that for one reason or another, you don't get a mortgage on the property. Now you must seek an uncollateralized loan—one for which there is no security other than your good name.

From a bank, an uncollateralized loan is going to be expensive and difficult to get, particularly if you want it for any big sum of money, say more than $10,000. It may take weeks to get, you will probably have to pay a higher interest rate than for a mortgage, and there may be an onerous repayment schedule. (At this point, some remodelers consider putting up some collateral, such as a paid-off car. Rest assured that the easiest collateral is real estate. After that, it's hard to put up collateral that the bank will consider worthwhile.)

Finally, if all else fails, many remodelers resort to paying for items on their credit card. They just charge the materials they need and get cash advances to pay for labor.

That's really expensive. Most credit cards these days charge about 20 percent in interest. If you need to borrow for a fairly long period of time, the interest charges alone could cause you to lose money on the deal.

In summary, the way to handle financing for any remodeling work, regardless of size, is to get it at the beginning. You should have a fairly accurate estimate of what your costs will be. (If not, go back and read the earlier chapters.) Now, arrange for the financing.

However you do it, get it done when you buy. Don't be like the chess player who never gets around to moving the bishop out of the back line and, as a result, has a weak game and often loses. Get your financing done up front.

Commonly Asked
Remodeling Questions

No home remodeling book would be complete without some help-ful hints. Here are questions about the field with answers that will save you the time it would otherwise take to learn about them.

No, the hints you find in here are probably not earth-shattering. But, if even one pans out for you, it could be a big time and money saver.

Why should I get a permit before remodeling?

I knew one remodeler who espoused the following philosophy: "I'll do all the work up to code, but I won't take out a permit. If I get caught, I'll have it inspected then. Otherwise, I don't have to hassle with inspections and fees."

My suggestion is that you don't follow this philosophy. My experi-ence with building departments is as follows. If there is work done that is not up to code, the building department will require it to be redone. That usually means ripping everything out to the bare bones so that the inspectors can see what's been done from the ground up.

Besides, saying that you're doing work to code without a permit is ridiculous. As anyone who has ever worked with a building depart-ment knows, many if not most of the rulings are arbitrary. What one inspector will pass, another will refuse. It's not whether the work is up to code that counts. It's whether you have that final inspection ticket that says the work was approved. Just because you think it's up to code doesn't mean an inspector will. If it helps, think of it as just another paper chase. You're after the slip of paper that gives you the building department's blessing.

Another point needs mentioning. It often doesn't cost any more to do it right than to do it slipshod. Yes, permit and inspection fees are high and getting higher. But often the inspector will suggest ways to accomplish something that you might not have considered, ways that could save money.

Finally, there's the matter of disclosure. The old days of *caveat emptor,* let the buyer beware, are long gone. In most states, when you sell, you must disclose any defects or problems in the property. This invariably includes any work done without a permit or inspection. If you fail to disclose, the buyer can later come back and demand rescission of the sale and damages. If you do disclose that work was done without a permit, many buyers will refuse to purchase. You're damned if you fail to disclose and damned if you do disclose when you don't have a permit.

Get a permit. Get it inspected. Avoid all kinds of nasty liability problems.

How do I get my plans done cheaply?

Plans are often the bane of remodelers. They may be excellent workers capable of doing a wide variety of chores, but when it comes down to plans, they feel helpless. I have seen people who would otherwise be excellent at remodeling forgo the field because they couldn't come up with an appropriate set of plans. Don't let a lack of plans defeat you. Draw them yourself, especially for small projects.

I have gone into building departments asking for permits with nothing more than sketches drawn on a notepad in pencil. I've never been thrown out. Most of the time, I've had to modify my drawings, but they have always been accepted eventually.

What's really important with a plan is to show exactly what you're going to do and how you're going to do it. Most people fail to include the details.

Say you're going to take out a wall and put in a passageway. You must show the structure of the walls, flooring, ceiling, roof and foundation as they currently are. You must also show the structure as it will be when finished. You should have details of headers and supports. You should show sizes of wood and where you're going to put metal flashing and braces.

If possible, you should also show load calculations. However, calculating loads has never been my forte, even though I have the various engineering books that give the appropriate values. What I usually do with a small job is try to figure the minimum sizes of supports and beams that I'll need, and then write that in the plans.

The engineers at the building department invariably go over the plans and check to see whether my calculations are correct. If not, they pencil in the correct sizes. In this way, I use the building department engineers to get my work done! Don't be too hasty to use this approach. Even if the building department approves your plans and you do the work, an on-site inspector can later say it's not up to code and make you change it. Furthermore, you always want to be sure that the materials used are at least up to minimum standards so that the building is safe. Therefore, if you have no personal knowledge of how to calculate sizes, have a structural engineer glance through your plans. For $50 to $100 the engineer will quickly give you the right information.

Where do I find bargains in building materials and supplies?

In an earlier chapter we talked about my Rule of the Single Purchase (if you need only one item, you can often get a bargain).

The question now, however, is how to find those bargains. You can't always count on getting just what you need when you need it at a discount. The answer is to always be looking. Once you actively become a remodeler, you must also become a detective. You must constantly be on the alert for bargains.

I never miss an opportunity to shop at a builder's supply or hardware store, particularly if it's one of the big discount outlets. I even walk through regular hardware stores checking to see what's on sale. (Sometimes regular hardware stores want to get rid of an item, or close it out, and will discount it 50 percent or more.)

I carry a little black book with me. In it I have two lists. The first contains all of the items I need for my current remodel project. The second is a generic list and contains items that I know I'll use one way or another over the course of the next couple of projects.

Whenever I see something that's a terrific buy, I flip out my little black book and check my lists. If the item is there, I buy it, even if I have to charge it on a credit card. I figure that as long as I know that I'll need it, I'm better off getting it now at a big discount than waiting until later and paying full retail.

Are there any special interior treatments that are cheap and look good?

There are all kinds. Here are a couple that you may find useful.

When it comes to window treatments in almost any room of the house, consider blinds. Blinds are available in metal and plastic, both in vertical and horizontal design. I prefer the plastic blinds because they are less subject to damage and more easily replaced, but metal blinds are considered more desirable.

At one time, blinds were one of the most expensive window treatments you could use. Recently, however, companies have developed ready-made blinds that you can buy in building discount stores. These blinds for a typical five-foot window often sell for less than $20! For a bit more you can purchase made-to-order blinds from many local shops or even discount warehouses.

My point is that blinds, very often, cost far less than traditional drapes or curtains, yet they carry an aura of class about them and they look good. My suggestion is to use blinds whenever possible.

With regard to lighting treatments, spend a little time checking out lighting stores as well as discount hardware stores. I always seem to find that they are discontinuing several kinds of lighting fixtures and have them on sale. If you can purchase an inexpensive but good-looking lighting fixture, you can then design the room around it.

Speaking of redesign, here's a helpful tip: Replace wallpaper; don't remove it and paint. As long as the existing wallpaper is securely stuck to the wall, it's far easier to put new paper on top of it than to attempt to peel it off and paint. There's even a special compound, sold under several brand names, that acts as a sealer on wallpaper and preps the surface. (Ask at your wallpaper/paint store.) If you attempt to peel the wallpaper, you'll find that it's difficult to get off. Once it's off, there will inevitably be a glue residue on the wall that itself is almost impossible to remove. Removing wallpaper and then painting is usually a much bigger job than you may first imagine.

If the existing wallpaper is loose, I try to glue it down securely. Again, this is easier than attempting to remove it. Only when the existing wallpaper is actually peeling, chipped or missing in spots will I take it off. And then I won't paint—I'll repaper the wall!

Finally, a word about carpeting. Carpeting is one of the most expensive items for the interior of the remodel home, yet good looking carpeting often sets the tone for the home. People very often judge the quality of the house by the quality of the carpeting.

Therefore, you are faced with a dilemma. You want a nice floor treatment, but you don't want to spend a great deal of money. One solution to consider is used (secondhand) carpeting.

Most people pull back when they first hear about this. "Used carpeting? You mean from someone else's house?" Well, yes, sort of. Often in very expensive homes, owners order carpeting and, once it is laid, decide they don't like it. They insist it be removed and be replaced with something else. It now becomes used carpeting and it is worth only a fraction of its original cost. It may have less than a month's worth of wear on it.

Sometimes offices or commercial buildings replace their carpeting. Usually they use only the top quality. Although most of what they throw out may be worn, often they replace so much that there are large areas that are almost new. You may be able to find enough top-quality carpeting in excellent condition to fit the bill for your remodel home from a commercial carpet replacement.

Keep in mind that although used carpeting is very cheap, usually only a couple of bucks per yard, it is also already cut up, which means you may have to buy many more yards, and it is trickier to lay.

Probably the most important consideration with used carpeting is not to be penny wise and pound foolish. The carpeting, ultimately, has to look good in the house. If it's the wrong color or a weird design, you shouldn't use it no matter how cheap it is. Only if it fits perfectly with the decor should you consider it. Sometimes cheap new carpeting will look good enough to catch a buyer's eye. Check with independent carpet jobbers in the yellow pages to find used carpeting.

How do I know what exterior style to give the house?

This is a question that is often puzzling to even the most experienced remodelers. Often the exterior appearance of the house is drab. Yes, new paint will help, but the house may simply be nondescript. There may be no curb appeal, nothing exciting or intriguing about its appearance. You want to spice it up, to make it call out to a potential buyer. How do you do that?

The answer is that you give the house style. Usually it's best to expand on the style it already has. There are a variety of different home styles, including, but not limited to, the following:

- Box

- Colonial

- Eastern brick

- Modern

- Prairie

- Tudor

- Victorian

- Western ranch

Each of these styles is distinctive and easily recognized. If you can't recognize a style, ask a couple of local agents. Almost always they can give you a clue as to what style the home actually is or was.

Once you've identified the underlying style of the home, exaggerate it. You can use different colors of paint to highlight the trim on Victorian houses. Adding a brick, wood or stone facade to a ranch can perk it up immensely. Try different-colored panels with a modern.

It's beyond the scope of this book to describe how to handle each style; however, you should be aware that there are numerous exterior style books illustrated with full-color pictures to give you ideas for improvement. They cover virtually every style imaginable. Check out your local bookstore or library for one that features the style of house you have and see what suggestions it offers.

One more comment is worth mentioning and that has to do with the first style I've listed here, box, which is not a style, but a description of a house without style. Usually the builder wanted to save money and used the cheapest design possible, which is a box design. You can recognize a box design because it has no character. Everything is symmetrical, and there is a flat, uninteresting front to the place.

What in the world do you do with a box style?

Consider adding a covered front porch. The only way to change the dull angles of a box design is to add on, and the cheapest way to add on is to add a porch. It will give the home new angles and will make it more interesting. Use interesting building materials for the porch, such as redwood or brick. A new porch can add life to an otherwise dead box design. (Once again, there are numerous books available on porch and deck design.)

How do I know if I need to add a room?

One obvious way to tell is if the house feels cramped when you walk around inside it. Another way to tell is by comparing the house to the norm. In this country the normal minimum-sized home is three bedrooms, two baths. Anything less than this, no matter how big the house may be in square footage, is considered less desirable, is less marketable and will bring a lower resale price.

Although the obvious answer may be adding another room, sometimes breaking through a wall between two rooms can give the airy, light feeling that's missing.

If the house has only one bathroom, consider adding another. If it has only two bedrooms, add another. You can be fairly sure when you do this that your addition makes sense.

A word about overbuilding: Even though adding another bedroom to a two-bedroom house adds to its value considerably, adding a fourth bedroom to a three-bedroom house does not. Similarly, adding a third bath to a two-bath house does not add enough to its value to justify the cost.

The rule is that your home should be up to minimum standards to make it easily marketable for a good price. You don't want to put more money into it for unnecessary additions than you can reasonably hope to get out.

Where's the best place to look for a good property to remodel?

That's a difficult question, given all the properties out there and the different locations around the country. Look for a small, old house in an area of largely custom-built (not tract) houses.

Here's my reasoning. Prices are difficult to nail down in custom-built areas. In a tract, the homes are identical and, as a consequence, it's easy to establish values. In a custom area, prices can vary enormously, often by $100,000, $200,000 or more.

In such an area, the older, smaller homes are typically the cheapest. Newer, larger homes command much higher prices. For example, a smaller run-down home built 60 years ago might be selling for $75,000. On the other hand, a newer, bigger and much more modern home might command a price in the $150,000 range.

I would buy the small, run-down house and remodel it, including adding on. Depending on my costs, if I could modernize the place and enlarge it, I could command top dollar on resale, around $150,000.

The reasoning here is that it's easier to find a good remodel house in this setting than to find a home sufficiently underpriced to make remodeling worthwhile in a tract. In a custom area, particularly if it's old and has been developed over a long period of time, often many such properties are available.

Index